THOUGHT LEADER LAUNCH

Entrepreneurship and Advertising
Nonprofit Management and Leadership
Small Business Sales and Selling

(September 2020)

Claim your free *Thought Leader Launch* starter library (video Masterclass, audiobook, ebook and more).

www.ThoughtLeaderLaunch.com

10 HABITS OF LEADERS

1. Leaders have a Massively Transformative Purpose.
2. Leaders take action.
3. Leaders are readers.
4. Leaders build teams.
5. Leaders read, write, and reflect.
6. Leaders build their brand.
7. Leaders generously help others.
8. Leaders have daily success habits.
9. Leaders are curious.
10. Leaders leave a legacy.

Suggestion: Post this where you will see it every day. Small actions, repeated consistently, will transform your life, business, and leadership!

Free *Thought Leader Launch* starter library—available for a limited time. Get your bonuses here today:

WWW.THOUGHTLEADERLAUNCH.COM

How To Get The Most Value From This Book

GET YOUR FREE *Thought Leader Launch* starter library here: www.ThoughtLeaderLaunch.com.

Implement the following 10 steps to enhance the value you receive from reading this book.

1. Leaders have a big, bold vision. What problems would you like to solve? What are you curious about? Clarify the legacy you intend to leave and the impact you want to make. This becomes your North Star. *Leaders have a Massively Transformative Purpose.*

2. What is the next step that will help you fulfill your Massively Transformative Purpose? Leaders take bold actions. Take some action every day toward achieving your goals. *Leaders take action.*

3. Reading is a superpower. Books contain the expertise and experience of the most successful people alive today—and the wisdom of those who have been dead for hundreds of years. Reading is the fastest way to get new ideas. Books are a way to be privately mentored by people who have already achieved the goals that are on your vision board. The right idea at the right time can be a game-changer. *Leaders are readers.*

4. Doing everything by yourself is kryptonite. Leaders leverage their own strengths, and delegate the rest. They don't waste their time floundering to do everything by themselves. Leaders surround themselves with smart, capable, competent people who are aligned with their vision. *Leaders build teams.*

5. Leaders generate ideas which enhance their life, business, and the world. They replenish their creativity by taking the time to read, write, and reflect. Reflect on what you are learning and write it down. By writing it down, you cement your key takeaways. Writing is thinking. *Leaders read, write, and reflect.*

6. Share your insights with others. Share the #1 thing you learned—or were reminded of—by reading this book. Sharing multiplies value. Please post a brief book review on Amazon or your favorite bookstore. You will be encouraging me to continue writing, and helping others discover this book. Thank you! *Leaders generously help others.*

7. Embrace new habits for 90 days and watch your life, relationships, and business transform! Practice the habits explained in this book, including: Radical Reading, Radical Writing, Radical Reflection, Meaningful Mornings, and these Leadership Habits. Tiny actions, repeated daily, are transformative. *Leaders have daily success habits.*

8. Your brand is not a logo. Your brand is your story—and the stories of the value you created for your clients. Knowing that business moves at the speed of trust, leaders build trust. They make it easy for people to "know, like, and trust them." Leaders attract premium opportunities with a strong brand. Without a valuable brand, a product or

service is a just a commodity—which means that the lowest price will win. *Leaders build their brand.*

9. Leaders look for new ways to add more value to their clients, coworkers, and community. They are open-minded, receptive, and innovative. *Leaders are curious.*

10. Leaders create impact. They leave the world a better place. They write books, give talks, and build businesses that make a meaningful difference. They share their expertise and experience, enriching the world. *Leaders leave a legacy.*

PRAISE FOR AURORA WINTER

"This well-written book serves up all of the ingredients one needs to get their message out, from soup to nuts. So pragmatic and direct—no fluff! For those of us starting a business, on the lecture circuit, or writing a book, Aurora is spot on. *Thought Leader Launch* has helped me immensely—staying on track and avoiding lots of pitfalls. A must read!!!"

– **Dr. Greg Hammer,** Professor, Stanford University School of Medicine

"I admire Aurora and her work. Others can gain strength from her wisdom and experience."

– **Dr. Bernie Siegel**, author *Love, Medicine, and Miracles*

"Do you have a message? Do you feel a desire to get that message out into the world? The only way to do that quickly, efficiently, effectively and successfully is to have a plan. Aurora gives you that plan and more. If you attempt it on your own, you may change a few lives, but if you follow the steps that Aurora lays in front of you, you can change the lives of hundreds of thousands—or millions—of people."

– **Robinson Smith**, author, *Master Your Mortgage and Retire Ready*

"Most people have no clue what a game-changer it is to become a published author. And becoming a media-savvy author is another quantum leap forward in influence, income, and impact. *Thought Leader Launch* is a must-read for anyone serious about becoming recognized as the leading expert in their field. It provides the insider info you need to succeed as an influencer today."

– **Alex Carroll**, best-selling author, media expert

"*Thought Leader Launch* is an epic book full of knowledge, wisdom, and tools to help you take action, overcome self-doubt, and use proven strategies to succeed. I highly recommend it! Keep it as your guide. It worked for me."

– **Irvana Eloundou, MBA**, Hotel owner

"This book is packed with hard-won wisdom to transform your leadership and business. A must-read for any leader wanting to maximize their influence and impact exponentially more lives. Aurora truly is an authority in helping Thought Leaders."

– **Mary Allen**, author, *The Power of Inner Choice*

"Thank you for your epic mentorship."

– **Dr. Tracy Thomas**, best-selling author, TEDx speaker

"*Thought Leader Launch* is a real paradigm shifter! It makes a very salient case for sharing my hard-earned knowledge and expertise for fun and profit. Aurora mixes lively writing, anecdotes, and on-message prescriptive seamlessly, sparking a bounty of ideas and providing clear direction. It is a blueprint for how to successfully launch as a Thought Leader."

– **Stephen Dedola**, business owner, LA

"I am thrilled to have found Aurora's book, which she has packed with hard-won wisdom that is already transforming my leadership skills and my business. *Thought Leader Launch* is a must-read for any leader who wants to live up to their full potential to influence and inspire."

– **Bruce McGovert**, entrepreneur, branding expert

"What a compelling and well written call to action for everyone to share their stories—with the guide for how to successfully get your message to your audience! I sat down with the intention of reading one chapter and got up almost 2 hours later after I finished it!"

– **Maureen Burke**, manager, Vancouver, WA

"Aurora Winter is a marketing expert who has launched three 7-figure businesses. She has a simple 3-step recipe you can use right away."

– **Jenny Toste**, anchor CBS-TV

"Aurora's stand for me—and for all of us—to truly find our niche, to find what our life has been a unique laboratory for, is truly awe-inspiring."

– **Gaile Burchill**, entrepreneur

"It is so important to create a clear, compelling message. And to systematize delivery to my customers in order to bring my gifts, skills, and talents to the world. I can't thank Aurora enough for how wonderful her content is!"

– **Bill Stierle**, entrepreneur

"Aurora Winter is a wonderful speaker and writer. Her content helps us go from stalled to stellar!"

– **Rev. Temple Hayes**, author
Intentional Spirit

"Do yourself a big favor and learn from this brilliant woman and master trainer."

– **James Malinchak**, author, featured
in ABC's *Secret Millionaire*

"Aurora's message is uplifting and empowering."

– **Mark Victor Hansen**, co-creator
Chicken Soup for the Soul series

"Get ready for a mind shift! People are hungry for transformation. *Thought Leader Launch* will help you transform into the leader you were meant to be."

– **Diane Burton**, author, TEDx speaker

"This book should be required reading in business school. Media can enhance your reputation and validate you as an expert in your field better than almost anything else. *Thought Leader Launch* reveals how anyone with valuable expertise can get their message out to the masses."

– **Steve Allen**, Founder, Steve Allen Media

"*The War of Art* meets *Influence*. Like Steven Pressfield, Aurora Winter encourages writers, and like Robert Cialdini, she layers in the psychology of influence and persuasion. *Thought Leader Launch* accelerated my career. Recommend."

-- **Timothy Forner**, author,
Montgomery Schnauzer, P.I.

THOUGHT LEADER LAUNCH

7 Ways to Make 7 Figures With Your

Million-Dollar Message

AURORA WINTER

BOOKS BY AURORA WINTER

- Thought Leader Launch
- From Heartbreak to Happiness
- Encouraging Words
- Grief Relief in 30 Minutes
- Grief Relief Workbook
- Chicken Soup for the Soul: Dreams and the Unexplainable *(contributing author)*
- GAIN Without Pain *(contributing author)*
- Marketing Fastrack

THOUGHT LEADER LAUNCH

Published by Same Page LLC
1750 Meridian Avenue, #4102
San Jose, CA, USA 95125

www.SamePagePublishing.com

ISBN 978-1951104009

This book is meant to strengthen your common sense, not to substitute for it. If legal advice or other expert assistance is required, the services of a competent professional person should be sought.

This book is not intended as a substitute for the advice of your doctor, lawyer, accountant, or any of your advisors, personal or professional.

Dedication

Dedicated to the first Thought Leader in my life, my mother, Dorothy Lawton.

She dared to think independently. When she wanted to go to university, her father informed her that she could be a teacher or a nurse. In the 1950s, those were the conventional norms for women.

She refused to be put into a small box and chose her own path. By stubbornly refusing to think small, and by speaking up to encourage others for decades, she did her part to create more opportunities for others, especially women. She was ahead of her time.

Thank you for your love and guidance, Mom.

I love you and miss you.

Aurora

April 19, 2020

Contents

10 Habits Of Leaders i

How To Get The Most Value From This Book ii

Foreword 1

Your Opportunity 5

Exponential Change 7

The Best of Hollywood & Silicon Valley 11

Leadership Tipping Point 15

1,000,000 Views & TEDx 22

Your Million-Dollar Message 25

Your Big Idea 25

Myth: Words Don't Matter 31

I Learned This The Hard Way—You Don't Have To 34

27× 38

Alt-MVP 39

Your Brand 45

You Don't Own Your Most Valuable Asset 45

How Oprah Built a Billion-Dollar Brand 47

Your Brand Is Your Story 48

Your Spotlight 55

You're Not In The Business You Think You're In 55

The 64/4 Rule 58

Neuroscience 59

Golden Spotlight 65

Your Business 69

Crossing the Chasm 70

Super Credibility 73

The New Transformation Economy 75

Your Million-Dollar Book 79
1. Attract Premium Clients & Premium Prices 83
2. Attract Investors, Launch Startup 89
3. TV or Movie Deal 91
4. Free Book & Upsell 94
5. Speaking 97
6. Training & Certification 99
7. Evergreen Bestseller 101

Your Launch 107
Million-Dollar Memoirs 109
Best-Selling Books 111
Your Platform 114
4 Phases to Launch 117
10-Step Launch Blueprint 120

Your Coach 127
Google CEO "Everyone Needs A Coach" 128
Talent Isn't Born. It's Grown. 129
How to Get a Million-Dollar Mindset...Fast! 137

Your Purpose 143
The Imposter Syndrome 156
Mindset 158
Procrastination 161
How to Avoid Regret 167

Your Turn 171
Thinking Is A Multiplier 172
Radical Reading, Writing & Reflecting 174
A Book Is Like Telepathy 178
Your Massively Transformative Purpose 179
Conclusion: Leadership Matters More Than Ever 188
Multiply Your ROI 193

10 Habits Of Leaders: Recap 196

About The Author 199

FOREWORD

"You're going to feel like hell if you wake up someday, and you never wrote the stuff that is tugging on the sleeves of your heart: your stories, memories, visions, and songs—your truth, your version of things—in your own voice. That's really all you have to offer us, and that's also why you were born."

~ Anne Lamott ~

THERE WAS SOMETHING wrong with me. I was too tired to watch our son, watch TV, or even read. (And I love reading books!) I was so exhausted it was a big decision to get off the couch to stumble the few feet to the nearby bathroom.

My husband, David, had hired a nanny to help me with our newborn. Still, instead of recovering, I was getting sicker and sicker. Finally, David made an appointment for me to see another doctor, this time, a specialist.

I went through a physical exam and a battery of tests. Waiting for the results was stressful. What was wrong with me? Did I have cancer? Was I going to die? I thought about the last few months that had led up to this moment in the doctor's office. After our son was born, I stayed home with him, overjoyed to have a beautiful baby boy—but I felt torn. I didn't want to let my husband down by turning my back on our thriving—but still fledgling—business.

Still, I was delighted to have some time to write finally. While my son was napping, I worked on the accounting for our business or worked on our marketing plans. When my son was awake, he was a handful, demanding my constant attention. My fantasy of writing while he was cooing in his playpen was just that—a fantasy. Instead, I got up at four in the morning to write.

However, instead of gradually recovering from the stress of childbirth and the intense early weeks of parenthood, I felt more and more depleted. Despite this, being a determined A-type personality, I pushed myself harder to be a great mom, wife, and business partner. I wrote in stolen moments before dawn.

My reflections were interrupted by the sound of a nurse calling my name. She ushered my husband and me into the doctor's office. Here was the moment of truth. My heart pounded. David held my small, cold hand in his big, warm one, reassuring me.

The doctor informed us that I had Epstein-Barr virus (known as "mono" or "yuppie flu").

"What's the treatment?" David asked.

"There's nothing I can do." The doctor explained that the virus would stay in my system forever. He thought I would probably start to feel better in a few months when the virus became dormant. However, the virus could become active again at any time.

This was sobering news. In the parking lot, my husband and I sat in our SUV, stunned. "You're doing too much," my husband concluded. "You don't have to work in our business anymore. I want you to write your book. But most of all, I want you to get better. I want you to decide right now that you're going to get well."

I looked into his concerned blue eyes and made a decision. Taking a deep breath, I declared, "Agreed. I'm going to get better, starting right now."

And I did. David had given me permission to honor the fact that my words and stories mattered. Once I carved out some daylight hours to write, I was amazed by how quickly I returned to my usual energetic, enthusiastic, optimistic self.

Through this experience, I discovered that there is a deep soul hunger—a deep need for self-expression, to share our stories, to be seen, to be heard. I had been suffering from a kind of soul sickness, trying to do enough to be worthy of love from others, yet neglecting to love myself. I had been telling myself disempowering stories—and I had made myself sick.

Living well is a creative act. We're all in this adventure called life together—and no one is getting out alive. Sharing your stories, insights, challenges, and triumphs with others is why you're here. I see it as a sacred contract. The way we thrive is by connecting and sharing what matters most. And that's not money.

In North America, we live in a culture obsessed with success, and where success is equated with money. However, studies show that after basic needs are met, there is little correlation between wealth and happiness. Yet, this myopic cultural delusion persists. Have we gone insane? It's time to reexamine what is meaningful.

When my Mother died in 2016, I cherished two things. The first thing I appreciated is that I was there when she took her last breath, just as she was there when I took my first breath. The second precious thing was the audio recordings I had made when I interviewed her, capturing her stories in her own words. I do not ever want to forget the details of the names, places, and insights she had gained from her childhood on the farm to her final years as the matriarch of our family. To me, this is deeply meaningful.

Stories create meaning. In the end, your life purpose is not your bank account. Your life story reveals rich layers of meaning. Sharing your story is the most significant thing you can do.

This book shares seven ways you can make seven figures with your Million-Dollar Message. The value of sharing your experience and expertise goes far beyond money. It is your life, your legacy. People are mortal. Books are not.

Capturing insights, epiphanies, challenges, and triumphs in a book is a proven way to broadcast your message. Your soul already knows that your experience and expertise matter. This book will serve to convince your neocortex—and your board of directors—that your book is a valuable asset. Like a magnet, your Million-Dollar Message attracts customers, income, and media coverage.

To share your message with the masses, it needs to be in a fixed form (such as a movie, video, podcast, audiobook, ebook, or book). Your message can then be broadcast to thousands—or millions— of people for virtually nothing, thanks to the internet.

Your experiences, expertise, and stories matter. Your stories may inspire movements, spark innovation, challenge preconceived notions, garner buy-in, and, most of all, create meaningful and valuable connections with others. Let's get started!

"The path to success is to take massive, determined action."

~ Anthony Robbins ~

1

YOUR OPPORTUNITY

"If you can read and think and communicate, you are absolutely 100% unstoppable. … There is nothing more economically valuable than teaching people how to communicate."

~ Jordan Peterson, professor, author ~

WHAT WILL CREATE a tipping point—what are the little things that will make a big difference? The right answer to this question can trigger a quantum leap. Failing to find the best solution can spell disaster, bankruptcy, or the slow death of mediocrity. If you are an entrepreneur or leader, you have likely grappled with this question, or its cousins, such as:

- How can we leap-frog past the competition—even if the competition is larger, more established, and better-financed?
- How can we get our message out to the masses—without spending a fortune on advertising?
- How can every sales call be tipped in our favor—even before the meeting begins?

- How can we get past the gatekeepers, stand out from the crowd, and access key decision-makers?
- What is the best way to attract affluent, pre-qualified clients?

These crucial questions confront business owners, leaders, and managers. The answers can make or break a product, service, launch, or business. To discover the best solutions for you, let's examine uber-successful entrepreneurs and decode their pathway to fame and fortune. Success leaves clues.

Elon Musk, Jeff Bezos, Sheryl Sandberg, Richard Branson, Arianna Huffington, Bill Gates, Oprah Winfrey, and other innovative thinkers have raised capital, raised awareness, launched startups, and launched movements. These bold disrupters used their creativity to grab our attention, knowing that without attention, even the best ideas wither and die. These extraordinary entrepreneurs are all recognized and rewarded as Thought Leaders.

As a serial entrepreneur, I know firsthand that launching and growing a business requires grit, determination, and persistence. Most founders grind away, putting in long hours to engineer their products and refine their services. But most leaders sabotage their success by failing to allocate 4% of their time to the one skill that delivers disproportionately-large results. Tragically, they are ignorant of the 64/4 Rule (more on that later).

Words triggered every lucrative leap forward in my life. Pitching or presenting my ideas, in books, in person, on stage, on TV, and on podcasts generated income and opportunity.

The power of storytelling is profound. People remember and repeat stories. We devour narratives of the setbacks and successes of people we admire.

Mel Robbins shared her paralyzing depression as her family faced bankruptcy. Her confidence was at an all-time low, and she could barely drag herself out of bed. The turning point came when she watched the countdown for a NASA launch. When her alarm went off the next morning, she did not press "snooze." Instead, she imagined the NASA countdown "5 … 4 … 3 … 2 …1!" and then launched herself out of bed. She leveraged this process to break self-destructive patterns and avert financial ruin.

When Mel Robbins shared her story in a TEDx talk, it resonated with people and went viral. That led to the creation of her book *The 5-Second Rule*, which rapidly became a bestseller. Riding this tidal wave of popularity, she became a sought-after speaker, and then the host of her own daytime TV talk show. Vision, passion, and purpose are magnetic when coupled with expertise, authenticity, and story-telling.

Like dandelion seeds, ideas float in the air. Whether they take root and grow—or wither and die—depends upon the message, messenger, and broadcast medium. People want authentic leaders who guide them towards greatness. People yearn to be part of something meaningful that is bigger than themselves.

If you would like to build a business, an organization, or a better future, this is an extraordinary time to be an influencer.

Exponential Change

THERE IS MORE opportunity—and more danger—than ever, due to exponential technological change. Understanding exponential change eludes most people. We tend to apply linear thinking, shrugging off the magnitude of divergence. Complacency is the road to ruin. Let me illustrate.

A long time ago, in a faraway land, an ingenious Inventor devised the game of chess. He presented it as a gift to the King. Delighted, the King invited the Inventor to name his reward. The Inventor asked for rice—a single grain of rice on the first square of the chessboard, two grains of rice on the second square, four on the third square, and so on, doubling each time. Scoffing at such a trivial reward, the King agreed.

How much rice do you think this would equal? Enough to fill a sack? A truck? A train?

When the Royal Treasurer attempted to pay the reward, he calculated that it was more rice than the entire kingdom possessed! By the time he got to the 64th square on the chessboard, there would be over 18 quintillion grains of rice on the board. To put that in perspective, that's about the number of animals living on planet Earth. Failing to understand exponential growth bankrupt the kingdom.

Most people are like the King in the fable—including CEOs, entrepreneurs, leaders, teachers, and politicians. The human brain is not wired to grasp exponential change. If you think like the Inventor, you can use this to your advantage. On the other hand, if you think like the King, exponential change could spell disaster.

Economist Joseph Schumpeter wrote about the paradox of "creative destruction." As entrepreneurs innovate, old ideas, technologies, and skills become obsolete. Progress means that society advances—but specific individuals may be worse off, not just in the short term, but forever. Pain and gain are inextricably linked with creative destruction.

How can leaders best respond to our rapidly-evolving world, rich with both danger and opportunity? How can emerging leaders influence the future to ensure a world that works for everyone? What are the best ways for you to benefit from this tidal wave of change?

Like a rising tide, exponential change impacts everything it touches, including our society, technology, and economy.

SOCIAL CHANGE

Technology is rewiring the way our brains work. Attention spans are shrinking. With an avalanche of content on social media every day, people are overwhelmed. As a result, people rely more and more on shortcuts to filter messages. These shortcuts include authority, status, and social proof.

Understanding and leveraging the neuroscience of communication gives leaders a distinct advantage. Attention hacks are more valuable than ever, including becoming a published author and appearing as a guest expert on podcasts and broadcasts.

ECONOMIC CHANGE

Thanks to exponential technological change, we have more lucrative opportunities than ever before. It is easier than ever to become a multi-millionaire—or even a billionaire—in a few short years. And the stakes have never been higher. The winners are companies like Facebook, Uber, Tesla, Netflix, and Google. One startup with just thirteen employees and only two years of operation under its belt was acquired for a billion dollars: Instagram.

Entrepreneurs in Silicon Valley are not waiting to discover the next unicorn—they are brainstorming ways to build it. However, many smart engineers and scientists have a blind spot—they are unable to articulate the value of their solution.

Entrepreneurs solve problems at a profit. The more significant and pervasive the problem, the bigger the potential profit. Clearly communicating value is essential to raising capital and enrolling customers, just as reaching the mass market is crucial to gaining market share.

Amazon has revolutionized small business by making advertising, shipping, and world-wide distribution seamless, inexpensive, reliable, and trusted. Amazon, eBay, PayPal, Stripe, YouTube, Eventbrite, Airbnb, FedEx, Facebook, Google, and other companies have made it feasible for small businesses—or even individuals—to profit from global demand. As a measure of Amazon's growing importance, it had almost half the US e-commerce market (260B USD) in 2018. A staggering 75% of Americans shop on Amazon. If your business involves some kind of expertise, you're missing out if you don't have a book showcasing your knowledge on Amazon.

TECHNOLOGICAL CHANGE

Amazon has changed the face of publishing, eroding the power of large publishers, and empowering authors and boutique publishers with print-on-demand publishing and easy world-wide distribution.

But writing hasn't gotten any easier. Sir Winston Churchill and other prolific, successful authors have discovered ways to make writing faster and easier. I will walk you through their creative strategies later in this book. In addition, you can access new technologies that Churchill didn't dream of. It is easier than ever to collaborate with expert wordsmiths, producers, designers, marketers, and mentors around the world.

The media landscape is rapidly changing. TED talks have created a valuable new platform for experts. Videos can go viral and reach millions of people. Mel Robbins shared her story and the 5-Second Rule on the TEDx stage, and that video now has over 20 million views! That is a staggering number of people to reach rapidly and virtually for free. New YouTube channels and new podcasts sprout like mushrooms, and they are eager to interview authors. In addition, radio, TV, and print media need tens of thousands of guest experts each and every **day** in America alone.

The Best of Hollywood & Silicon Valley

I LIVE IN Silicon Valley, but my roots are in Hollywood. Both of these places are more about mindset than geography. Silicon Valley is about startups and capturing market share. Hollywood is about story-telling and capturing attention.

Fusing the best elements from both places produces a path to prosperity, prestige, and prominence. This highway is overlooked by the lion's share of engineers, scientists, and other smart, analytical people. If you are smart and ambitious, you don't want to neglect this potential tipping-point.

To see if the Thought Leader strategy is a good fit for you and your business, charity, or organization, you need the answers to some important questions, including:

- Do you have what it takes to become a Thought Leader?
- What skills and assets are required?
- Should you self-publish or go the traditional route?

- What does it take to create a best-seller?
- How can you write a book if you're not a writer?
- What if you don't have any time to write, or you're not sure what to write about?
- Has anyone ever sold a million copies of their self-published book in a year?
- What kinds of businesses profit the most from leadership positioning?
- What qualities make a leader unforgettable?
- How can you follow a proven blueprint for success?

My goal is to answer these questions in this book. That way, you can see if the Thought Leader strategy is a good fit. If so, you will want to build the team, skills, and assets you will need to thrive as a media-savvy visionary-author–speaker-entrepreneur. In this book, I've shortened this multi-faceted role to "Thought Leader."

When Thought Leaders combine the best of Hollywood's show-biz with the best of Silicon Valley's smarts, they are frequently delighted by the amazing results. Even a little "celebrity stardust" can make a world of difference.

For example, my clients Drs. Justene and Janice Doan tripled their 7-figure dentistry practice after we produced and published their book, *Keys to a Healthy Smile After 40*, which positioned them as the only logical choice for their ideal patient. (More on that success recipe later.) As self-made billionaire W. Clement Stone said, "little hinges swing big doors." Words are those little hinges.

What does this mean for you? It means that the right words, at the right time, to the right people can change your life. It can change your income, your impact, and your future, as it did with me.

MY FIRST TELEVISED PITCH

Fresh out of college, my husband and I were newlyweds. We were madly in love, so we started a business. We had no idea how to run a business, but we were determined to be together. That little business that we started with so much love grew to be a seven-figure business selling sailboats and powerboats.

I remember one Christmas we had a $1 million **cash** in our business bank account! Wow! That was incredible for two kids in our twenties. We looked at each other and grinned. "Should we run away to the Bahamas?" Of course, we would never do that, but it was gratifying to be trusted with so much cash just a few years after we had been struggling to keep the lights on and the doors open.

John Badham (who directed the movie *Stakeout*) had rented one of our yachts to film the movie *Bird on a Wire*. My husband was the captain, and I was the crew during the day of filming. So we had the opportunity to connect with John Badham, Mel Gibson, Goldie Hawn, and Peter Marshall. As a result of that connection, I was hired and paid for the first time to write a screenplay. It was a nominal amount of money, but I was ecstatic to be a paid professional.

I devoted myself to writing and launching my new career. Meanwhile, my husband sold our yacht sales business and focused on building our dream home. We had cash in the bank and the freedom to do what we wanted. Life was good and about to get even better! Or so I thought.

But then, my thirty-three-year-old husband dropped dead suddenly, for no apparent reason, right in front of me. I was devastated.

My entire life shattered. I felt like Humpty-Dumpty, smashed into hundreds of pieces. I had no idea if I could ever super-glue the pieces of my life back together again. Sometimes I despaired. But I had a compelling reason to try—our four-year-old son.

Besides the unthinkable tragedy of having lost my young husband, I had other pressing problems. I didn't have a job. I didn't have my business partner. I didn't have my husband and best friend. But I **did** have an urgent need to provide for my little family of two. I was suddenly a single mom. And a widow—how I despised that word.

Not long after my husband's death, I was invited to pitch my screenplay at the Banff Television Festival (now called the Banff World Media Festival). This could be my big break. I could pitch my movie idea to six hundred of the "movers and shakers" in Hollywood and around the world. This could make a world of difference and launch my career.

Or it could go the other way, and I could ruin my reputation forever. If people weren't in the room during my presentation, they could always watch it later on television. A documentary filmmaker was going to film my 20-minutes on stage in the spotlight.

I practiced. I polished. And then ... I pitched.

It went even better than I thought it possibly could. My agent fielded offers on my behalf. My talk sparked a bidding war, launched my career in film and television, and generated six figures. It changed my reputation and made me a little bit famous in my industry.

My pitch aired on national television as the documentary *The Big Break* and later was used to teach the art of pitching at the Banff Film School.

That one pitch changed the trajectory of my life—a pretty colossal result for a single twenty-minute presentation. The right words at the right time to the right people can produce a massive outcome.

Leadership Tipping Point

THE WORDS OF Ray Dalio, Steve Jobs, Bill Campbell, Mary Kay, Lee Iacocca, Katharine Graham, Sam Walton, Wayne Dyer, and Sir Winston Churchill immortalize their authors.

Ideas that might otherwise have been forgotten become part of our social and economic landscape because they have been committed to the page. A book can intimately influence people now—and long after the author is gone.

Today, the next generation of innovators is eager for their own disruptive ideas to be embraced by the mass market. But the majority of people distrust change—only 16% of the market is receptive to new ideas.

However, one proven way to appeal to the public is to broadcast your views on mass media channels that are respected in your industry, and, of course, through books.

Books build trusted leaders. Books launch businesses and movements. A book cannot provide the same insights as individual training and mentoring. Still, it can spark reflection, reveal new possibilities, and provide a roadmap. I aim to do just that in this book.

Thought Leader Launch distills my experience training, mentoring, and media-coaching entrepreneurs, as well as my own expertise as an entrepreneur, author, TV producer, and publisher. I will share the strategies that my clients and I have successfully used to reach, raise, and make millions.

We will cover:

- Your Million Dollar-Message
- Your Brand
- Your Spotlight
- 7 Ways to Make 7 Figures
- Your Thought Leader Launch Blueprint
- Your Mentor & Mastermind
- Your Legacy

I recommend that you jot down your ideas, and insights as you read this book.

To get you started, consider these questions:

- What do you need to tell prospects repeatedly?
- What do you wish you had known earlier?
- What lessons would you like to share with your grandchildren?
- How do you make decisions?
- What makes you angry?
- What is the biggest challenge you have faced?
- How did you overcome this challenge—or even grow wiser as a result?
- What is the biggest myth you'd like to bust in your industry?

The Thought Leader Launch strategy can be a tipping point for your leadership and legacy. I hope you use it to broadcast ideas worth sharing and build a world that works for everyone.

Let's look at a few examples of entrepreneurs who have built and enhanced their brands and businesses by becoming published authors.

SIR RICHARD BRANSON: THE VIRGIN WAY

Sir Richard Branson commands media attention. He founded the Virgin Group Ltd., which controls over 400 companies and has more than 70,000 workers. In 2018, Branson's net worth was estimated to be $5 billion. His oversized personality and flowing blond locks are custom-made for a sound-bite era.

Branson has written a shelf's worth of books, including:

- *Like a Virgin: Secrets They Won't Teach You at Business School*
- *Losing My Virginity: How I Survived, Had Fun, and Made a Fortune Doing Business My Way*
- *Finding My Virginity: The New Autobiography*
- *The Virgin Way: If It's Not Fun, It's Not Worth Doing*

Notice that the Virgin brand is embedded in the title of each of his books. Branson is no media neophyte—he understands that books trigger valuable media coverage. Given his business philosophy, Branson would not write so many books if it wasn't fun—and profitable. However, Branson is dyslexic. Reading and writing have been major stumbling blocks throughout his life. So how can writing books be fun for him?

He made it enjoyable by creating books with the right team. Branson's books contain his thoughts, stories, and philosophy, but he's not the one doing the tedious copyediting, fact-checking, and proof-reading. He has mastered the art of delegation. Instead,

Branson provides the content, and hires others to transform that content into an engaging and entertaining book.

ARIANNA HUFFINGTON: THRIVE

Ariana Huffington became recognized as a Thought Leader by broadcasting her ideas in blogs and books. She founded *The Huffington Post* in 2005, and it quickly became one of the most widely-read internet media brands. In 2012, the site was honored with a Pulitzer Prize for national reporting. *The Huffington Post* was acquired by AOL for $315 million. Huffington enhanced the value of her brand and platform through ongoing communication, and in the process, made herself rich. Her net worth was estimated at $50 million in 2019.

Her books include:

- *Thrive: The Third Metric to Redefining Success and Creating a Life of Well-Being, Wisdom, and Wonder*
- *On Becoming Fearless...in Love, Work, and Life: A Road Map for Women*
- *The Sleep Revolution: Transforming Your Life One Night At A Time*

Honored as one of the world's 100 most influential people by *Time* magazine, Huffington does not waste her time struggling with writing. Instead, she dictates her thoughts. Like Branson, Huffington delegates.

JASON CALACANIS: ANGEL

Books can help promoters—like Branson—sell. But books can also attract investors. As the founder of an investment syndicate, Jason Calacanis wants a steady flow of the best early-stage investment opportunities.

His book, *Angel: How to Invest in Technology Startups—Timeless Advice from an Angel Investor Who Turned $100,000 into $100,000,000*, attracts early-stage investment opportunities.

Calacanis has invested in seventy-four companies, including the unicorns Thumbtack, Calm, and Uber. As a result, Calacanis has multiplied the value of his investments a thousand-fold.

HOWARD SCHULTZ: A BILLION-DOLLAR BOOK?

Starbucks generated $22 billion in 2017, twenty-seven times more than the $800 million generated by Peet's Coffee in 2016. (A little later, I'll share research that validates the "27×" value of a good story.)

Howard Schultz, the former CEO and Chairman of Starbucks, has written several books, including:

- *Pour Your Heart Into It: How Starbucks Built a Company One Cup at a Time*
- *Onward: How Starbucks Fought for Its Life Without Losing Its Soul*
- *From the Ground Up: A Journey to Reimagine the Promise of America*

How much of Starbucks' $20 billion-dollar advantage is because Howard Schultz is an author and Thought Leader who enjoys the media spotlight? It is hard to know for sure, but certainly Starbucks benefited from the publicity.

So did Schultz. Confident on-camera, he tossed his hat in the ring for a brief time as a 2020 Presidential candidate. His net worth was estimated at $4 billion USD in November of 2019.

BOOKS LAUNCH MOVEMENTS

Malala Yousafzai sparked an international campaign for the education of girls. Her book, *I Am Malala: The Girl Who Stood Up for Education and Was Shot by the Taliban*, fueled outrage. The ongoing media coverage triggered a global reaction, and Malala became the youngest-ever Nobel Prize laureate.

Sheryl Sandberg's book, *Lean In: Women, Work, and the Will to Lead*, produced a movement, a popular TED talk, and countless media appearances.

Marie Kondo's popular movement "sparks joy" as people de-clutter. Her book, *The Life-Changing Magic of Tidying Up: The Japanese Art of Decluttering and Organizing*, also sparked a Netflix series. Kondo visits the homes of the hopelessly disorganized and helps them gain control of their clutter—and their lives.

BOOKS BUILD TRUST

Business moves at the speed of trust. People are inundated with information. Buyers need a way to make decisions quickly, without getting bogged down in a mountain of data. Buyers assess who they "know, like, and trust" with shortcuts including status, expertise, and familiarity.

Robert Cialdini, the author of *Influence*, the classic book on the psychology of persuasion, recently published a follow-up book, *Pre-suasion*, which emphasizes the importance of what happens **before** the first meeting. Your reputation precedes you. Your book and media appearances establish a frame of expertise and authority. Framing profoundly impacts decisions, as Nobel Prize winner Daniel Kahneman detailed in *Thinking, Fast and Slow*.

In his excellent book *Pitch Anything*, Oren Klaff states that setting the frame—or frame control—is the decisive factor in any pitch or presentation. In framing, status is paramount. Books enhance star power.

BOOKS BUILD LEADERS

So far, we've established that a book can boost your business, brand, and bottom line. It develops trust and authority. A book strengthens leadership capabilities. Your book is an extension of your philosophy, your values, and your personality.

Your book cultivates what I call the 10 C's:

1. Capability
2. Creativity
3. Credibility
4. Celebrity
5. Connections
6. Charisma
7. Character
8. Clarity
9. Certainty
10. Confidence

The process of writing your book—or being interviewed so that your team or ghostwriter can write your book—enhances your clarity, creativity, and confidence. Confidence and clarity are magnetic leadership qualities.

Your book can expand your persuasiveness, power, and poise. It can help you reach millions.

1,000,000 Views & TEDx

I met Louise Evans a few years ago when we both attended a nine-day workshop on *Non-Violent Communication* given by the late, great Marshall Rosenburg. Then, as now, she was polished, caring, and committed to life-long learning, whether from Marshall Rosenburg, or the University of Cambridge.

"We spend about eighty percent of our day at work, the rest is at home," Louise said. "If we have a bad day at work, we are likely to take that negativity home with us and vice versa. It is of paramount importance that we create healthy environments in the spaces that most affect our lives by giving our best and receiving the like in return."

Louise successfully transformed the workplaces where she delivered her unique brand of training, but widespread negativity in other corporations weighed on her heart. She knew she could make a bigger impact if only she could reach a broader audience. So, in 2016, she self-published her book *5 Chairs, 5 Choices: Own Your Behaviours, Master Your Communication, Determine Your Success*.

Her decision to write and publish her book was the first tipping point. The book was well-received, and she was invited to give a TEDx talk in Genova, Italy. After extensive rehearsal, she delivered that talk in 2017—and it created the second tipping point.

In her TEDx talk, Louise revealed both her expertise and her humanity. She confessed her desire to befriend Samira, the young woman who would soon become her daughter-in-law. Despite Louise's best efforts to connect, Samira ignored her, preferring to text on her cell phone. Distressed, Louise agonized over how to respond. Using this compelling story as a framing device, Louise shared the different thinking styles of her *5 Chairs, 5 Choices* system, applying each one to this sticky situation.

This relatable story struck a chord with viewers. The video of her TEDx talk rapidly attracted 700,000 views, and she found herself with more business than she knew how to handle. That's when she came to me for strategic planning.

The increased demand for her expertise meant that she could scale her business. She is now training and certifying coaches to deliver her popular *5 Chairs, 5 Choices* method. She is creating online video training to leverage her time. As a newlywed in her sixties, she values spending time with her husband.

"Aurora helped me leverage the success of my popular TEDx talk to grow my business, team, impact, and influence," Louise wrote. "Aurora Winter is a very strategic, creative, innovative thinker."

At our Thought Leader Mastermind retreat in Florence May 2019, Louise enthusiastically shared that her TEDx talk had attracted over 1,400,000 views. Our entire Mastermind group cheered, celebrating that her video has gone viral. Louise has successfully launched a movement, thanks to one self-published book and one TEDx talk.

VIRAL VIDEOS

TED talks were viewed 125 million times every month in 2016. TED talks are typically 18 minutes long, a sweet spot for holding attention while still exploring a topic in some depth. People watch over a billion hours of YouTube videos every single day—and the average viewing session on YouTube is more than 40 minutes.

More than 1,000 TED speakers have reached over 1,000,000 views for a *single* speech, according to Chris Anderson, the curator of TED. In his book, *TED Talks,* Anderson puts 1,000,000 views in context. "Over history, many of the people passionate about an idea have spent years crisscrossing a country or a continent trying to drum up audience interest."

A speaker with an outstanding PR machine and a grueling schedule might speak 100 times a year to audiences of 500 each time, resulting in reaching 50,000 people after a year. Compare this number to how many people you can reach online in a single **day**. Anderson wrote, "This represents a transformative leap in influence, and many speakers have attested to the impact it has made on their work."

Videos are memorable. According to research published by Facebook, people remember videos at a statistically significant rate after viewing only .25 seconds! As a result, videos play an important role in marketing.

When I launched a new offer recently, I used one of my books as a lead magnet, then followed up with a sequence of five videos. That generated $250,000 of new business in 90 days—without a big launch, joint venture partners, or any full-time employees.

A book can establish your expertise, experience, and enthusiasm. Videos continue the process of building trust and adding value.

Next, let's dive into the art and architecture of creating and broadcasting your own unique Million-Dollar Message.

"If we did all the things we are capable of doing, we would literally astound ourselves."
~ Thomas A. Edison ~

2

YOUR MILLION-DOLLAR MESSAGE

"The pen is mightier than the sword."
~ EDWARD BULWER-LYTTON ~

Your Big Idea

YOU'VE GOT THE best idea since the creation of the internet. It's going to change the world. It's a BIG IDEA.

But you need funding. You need investors, you need clients, you need a five-star team, you need to get the word out.

Your Big Idea is like a 747 sitting on the tarmac at LAX without any fuel. That fuel is your magnetic message. Without it, you can't take off.

You need the right message. Something that will cut through the noise in the marketplace. Something that will grab our most precious resource—no, not money. Attention.

Attention is finite. We each have only 24 hours each day. In a world where people are constantly bombarded with messages, your Big Idea needs a clear, compelling, concise message.

Studies show that the human attention span has shrunk to 5 seconds. Can you convey your big idea in 5 seconds?

What is a "Million-Dollar Message"? It can take many forms, but it must include a clear vision and a compelling message.

A determined, resourceful, committed entrepreneur who has mastered the right Million-Dollar Message is practically unstoppable. This book will help you discover and then hone that message so you can go big, create wealth, and impact the world. You will learn winning moves to attract capital, clients, and media coverage, even if you are like David, and your competition is like Goliath. Even if most people think your idea is impossible. Even if—especially if—you want to improve the world. You will also meet some of my clients, who are extraordinary entrepreneurs and leaders. I will share the proven five-step formula my clients and I have used to reach, raise, and make millions.

It all starts with a Million-Dollar Message, a clear, concise, bold idea that sparks the imagination, like Bill Gates' vision of a computer on every desk and in every home. At the time, this was a revolutionary idea.

"It was a bold idea, and a lot of people thought we were out of our minds to imagine it was possible," Gates wrote. "It is amazing to think about how far computing has come since then, and we can all be proud of the role Microsoft played in that revolution."

Steve Jobs could not spark a movement by echoing the same idea. But he launched a billion-dollar company and a buying frenzy when he showcased the iPod as "a thousand songs in your pocket."

Million-Dollar Messages are powerful and demand attention. They can leverage the unexpected, like Seth Godin's "purple cow," or the paradoxical like Brené Brown's "power in vulnerability." They can leverage controversy, like Donald Trump's wall. A Million-Dollar Message distills an idea to its essence. Examples of this kind of distillation abound, including:

- "The Four-Hour Work Week" (Tim Ferriss)
- "Power in Vulnerability" (Brené Brown)
- "People Don't Buy What You Do. They Buy Why You Do It" (Simon Sinek)
- "Purple Cow" (Seth Godin)
- "A Thousand Songs in Your Pocket" (Steve Jobs, launching the iPod)
- "Women in the Workforce Need to Lean In" (Sheryl Sandburg)
- "A Computer on Every Desk and in Every Home" (Bill Gates)
- "We Will Build a Wall and Mexicans Will Pay for It" (Donald Trump)
- "For Every Pair of Shoes Sold, a Pair Given to a Child in Need" (Blake Mycoskie, TOMS shoes)
- "Girls Must Have Access to Education" (Malala Yousafzai)
- "Transforming Cars to Run on Electricity" (Elon Musk)

To learn more about how to create your own Million-Dollar Message, watch the bonus video *Bill Gates Used This Key, And You Can, Too*: www.thoughtleaderbonuses.com.

Like these great thinkers, my clients and I have used clear, concise, compelling messages to reach, raise, and make millions. Because of thoughtful crafting of these messages, I have benefited from millions of dollars of free publicity being a guest expert on TV and radio, including FOX, CBS, NBC, Oprah radio, *Success* magazine, *Elle* magazine, and more.

Now, I don't know you, and I don't know your skills, background, or the quality of your backbone. My results are not typical. My clients are extraordinary leaders and entrepreneurs. Their results are not typical, either. However, I believe success is inevitable with the right message, mindset, skills, and determination. And that depends on you.

Having a Million-Dollar Message is more important than ever. Here's why. Things have changed. The Information Economy is dead. The Transformation Economy is here. Exponential change is happening now, whether you like it or not, and the pace of change is accelerating.

There will be big winners and big losers. The big losers will be complacent. There is no standing still in our rapidly-changing world. If you coast, you're toast. More on exponential change later. Here's the bottom line for entrepreneurs—evolve or die.

The big winners will have a big, bold vision of how they can contribute to the world, and they will declare it with a clear, convincing, concise Million-Dollar Message. The winners will be Thought Leaders.

Here's the paradox—the best ideas are the most challenging to convey to others—because they disrupt entire industries and bring exponential change, not mere incremental change. And our human brains don't readily comprehend exponential change.

HELL—WITHOUT THE RIGHT MESSAGE

If people don't see, understand, and embrace your vision, it is hell for an innovative leader or entrepreneur. Not being understood creates a negative feedback loop and a downward spiral.

The messenger becomes less and less confident, certain, and charismatic. Immediate consequences can include:

- Frustration
- Uncertain
- Rambling
- Not clear
- Not confident
- Ineffective
- Being misunderstood
- Weak
- Shame
- Despair
- Downward spiral

When people don't see, understand, and buy into your vision, it can have devastating long-term business and personal consequences, such as:

- Not attracting investors
- Not enrolling clients
- Not attracting top talent
- Panic as you run out of runway (cash)
- The pain of not living up to your full potential
- Fear about the future
- Anxiety about your retirement
- Stress eroding your health and vitality
- Strained relationship with your spouse

- Compromised relationships with your family, friends, and community
- The pain of not leaving a legacy
- Your brilliant idea is stillborn
- Bankruptcy

HEAVEN—WITH THE RIGHT MESSAGE

In contrast, it is heaven when you have your own unique Million-Dollar Message (such as Bill Gates' "a computer on every desk" or Steve Jobs' "a thousand songs in your pocket").

When people see, understand, and embrace your vision, it creates an upward spiral of positive momentum.

The messenger becomes more and more:

- Confident
- Certain
- Clear
- Charismatic
- Attractive
- Effective
- Enthusiastic
- Prized
- Proud
- Powerful

BENEFITS

When people align with your vision, it has tangible benefits. Other people are typically eager to jump on board in meaningful ways, such as:

- Cash from investors
- Cash from new clients
- Buzz from media coverage
- Top talent attracted to your team
- Milestones achieved
- Fortune 500 companies invest or joint venture
- Value of your company shoots up
- Increased wealth and net worth
- Opportunities come chasing you
- A meaningful, prosperous, secure future is assured
- Prosperity
- Contribution
- Significance
- Explosive growth
- Lucrative buyout
- Leaving a legacy—to contribute to your family
- Leaving a legacy to enrich the world

In a minute, I will give you some practical examples to inspire you to create your own Million-Dollar Message. But first, I need to bust a myth.

Myth: Words Don't Matter

FACT: WORDS CREATE reality.

1. First, you see it
2. Then you say it
3. Then you have it

1. FIRST YOU SEE IT

It all starts with your vision. People want to align with a vision greater than themselves. Proclaim your vision!

"Where there is no vision, the people perish." – *Proverbs*

People are hungry to follow a leader with a vision: Bill Gates, Steve Jobs, Elon Musk, Sheryl Sandburg, Malala Yousafzai, Oprah.

Your vision is like a blueprint for building a house. First, you see it in your mind's eye. Everything is twice created. The first creation is your vision.

2. THEN YOU SAY IT

Declaring your vision is potent. First, there was the word. Then there is the manifestation.

"God said, "Let there be light." And there was light." – *King James Bible*

Your words have the power to create. Declare the future you want to see.

3. THEN YOU HAVE IT

Bill Gates and Steve Jobs transformed the world with their vision for the future. They created a new reality.

Here are some more examples of entrepreneurs who created massive value in the world—and in their businesses—by having a clear vision and a clear message.

TOMS Shoes

"Sell a pair of shoes today, give a pair of shoes tomorrow," is the simple, powerful concept of TOMS Shoes founder

Blake Mycoskie. As a result, they have given away 95 million pairs of shoes!

Zappos

Tony Hsieh's vision was to "Wow customers." The goal is to deliver happiness, not just shoes. One Zappos employee provided a caller with the requested list of nearby pizza places. Another spontaneously ordered flowers for a customer whose husband had died in an accident. These are just two examples of going above and beyond standard customer service.

Google

The unofficial mission statement of Google is, "Don't be evil." Founder Larry Page said, "We have a mantra: don't be evil, which is to do the best things we know how for our users, for our customers, for everyone. So I think if we were known for that, it would be a wonderful thing." Now that the power of search algorithms and big data is becoming fully apparent, this commitment to not being evil is more valuable than ever.

Tesla

Elon Musk has never been accused of dreaming small dreams. "Transforming all cars to run on electricity" is his vision. He's given his valuable patents away to competitive car manufacturers to support his long-term vision. As a result, we are decades closer to cleaning up air pollution and making our world a healthier place for generations to come.

I Learned This The Hard Way—You Don't Have To

I LEARNED ABOUT the value of a Million-Dollar Message the hard way. My business is thriving now, but it wasn't always that way. There were a lot of sleepless nights to learn the things that I'm going to share with you.

I met David, the man who was to become my husband, at university, where we were both studying economics. Fresh out of university, we each got corporate jobs. But we were so madly in love we couldn't stand to be apart.

So we decided that the solution was to start a business together. But what business could we start with no money?

WHAT COULD POSSIBLY GO WRONG?

We quit our jobs with the joyful abandon of two kids who have no idea how difficult it is to launch a new business. I remember the first boat show we attended. The competition dismissed us as irrelevant, sneering that "those kids won't be back to the next boat show."

They came close to being right. At first, we were cocky and confident. Next, we were determined to prove the competition wrong. Then we ran out of cash. Humiliated, we claimed unemployment insurance to keep groceries on the table. My husband got a job to keep the lights on. We were struggling to stay afloat.

One day, I noticed that rental apartment buildings had huge tax shelter benefits in British Columbia, Canada, at that time.

I asked the million-dollar question, "I wonder if we could do that with boats?" People told us that we couldn't. But after spending $20,000 with lawyers and accountants, we discovered the answer was that we could, in fact, provide tax shelter benefits.

This was a million-dollar IDEA. But we still didn't have a Million-Dollar MESSAGE.

In my enthusiasm, I buried prospects with way too much information, with Income Tax (IT) bulletins from Revenue Canada, with excel spreadsheets, marginal tax rates, and details on the 7% investment tax credit and 33 1/3% straight-line depreciation (subject to the half-year rule in the first year). By setting up a boat rental business for each of our clients and structuring the boat as 90% for business use, 90% of the expenses of boat ownership could be legitimately deducted. The substantial tax benefits slashed the net cost of owning a boat.

Prospects glazed over and left, confused by the avalanche of information. I knew it was a winning idea. But unless I could convey that idea, our little business would be out of cash.

How could I get the message across?

After some trial and error, I finally came up with a message that made the phone ring.

WINNING MESSAGE

Five weeks of sun, fun & tax shelter

That caught people's attention, especially when it was coupled with a photo of a sleek sailboat and people having fun on vacation.

That Million-Dollar Message created massive results:

- Millions of dollars in yacht sales
- Generating $3,000,000 of new orders at a boat show in just one week
- Doubling profit margins (from 12% to 24%)
- Attracting media coverage (*BC Business* magazine featured us on the cover)
- Becoming the largest yacht dealer in Western Canada

Here's another example from another one of my businesses—a film and television production company. I realized that an innovative business structure would set the company up for success and differentiate it from larger, more established, and better-capitalized competition. I proudly put the finishing touches on a thick business plan. But that business plan simply provided the "thud" factor to accompany this Million-Dollar Message:

Maximize film funds, grants, and tax benefits from the UK, Canada, and the Isle of Mann

As a result, that startup company raised approximately $5,000,000 and got the funds needed to produce eight films (and counting).

My husband died at the age of thirty-three when our son was only four. I was devastated. I spent years learning how to overcome grief and rebuild my life.

My first book, *From Heartbreak to Happiness: An Intimate Diary of Healing*, shared my journey. It was endorsed by Dr. Wayne Dyer, who wrote, "I read every page of this beautiful diary—it touched my heart, and I'm sure it will impact yours."

My message of hope was simply, "If I can go from heartbreak to happiness, you can, too." The book was my gift to grieving people, and I intended to go back into the film business.

But people wanted more. They kept asking me, "How did you get happy again? How can I overcome grief like you did?"

I began coaching a few people through grief. In the same week, two of my clients said practically the same thing, "You helped me more in that one session than my therapist has helped me in months—and I have a good therapist. Can you teach me how to do the same?"

When I get the same message twice, I pay attention. So I said, "Sure" and founded the Grief Coach Academy, which is devoted to training coaches to help people go from heartbreak to happiness more quickly and easily.

At the time, therapists and the coaching establishment dismissed the Grief Coach Academy as irrelevant, sneering that it was not possible to coach someone through grief—convinced that grieving people needed therapy. I had plenty of evidence that they were wrong. But I didn't waste my breath trying to convince the establishment.

Instead, I took my message to the media. Here's the empowering message that launched the Grief Coach Academy:

Grief is a normal and natural reaction to loss. Typically, people suffer from 5 – 8 years. That is way too long! With the right coaching, people can recover 10x faster.

27×

CAN A STORY increase the value of an item? If so, by how much?

The book *Significant Objects: 100 Extraordinary Stories About Ordinary Things* shared an experiment which contrasted the value of 100 different objects offered for sale on eBay, either with a story or without.

The descriptions were not hyping the value of each product, but added a layer of significance. For example, the product detail might share that these particular pot mitts were owned by the seller's grandmother, and fond memories of the chocolate chip cookies that she baked. A number of writers provided the anecdotes, some writers were professionals and others were amateurs. Some of the narratives were even negative!

The stories increased the meaning of the object—but would that impact the selling price? The result was 27× more revenue, increasing the overall value from $128 to $3,612! That would be analogous to a stock value increasing from $.07 to $1.89—with the right story.

The product stayed precisely the same. Words increased value by 2,700%. Wow.

Neglecting the value of the story is leaving money on the table—a LOT of money.

Alt-MVP

SILICON VALLEY IS overflowing with incredibly smart engineers, and scientists focused on the Next Big Thing. But their brilliant ideas will be stillborn unless other people can see their vision.

Silicon Valley is a mindset, not a place. It's a disruptive startup culture. When I talk about "Silicon Valley," I'm talking about an ambitious, entrepreneurial, creative, bold mindset.

Many tech companies exhaust their resources attempting to perfect their MVP (Minimum Viable Product). In my experience, they would be much better off focusing on an alt-MVP (Masterful Visionary Pitch). If investors do not understand the problem you solve and value of that solution, your startup will not get funded—no matter how elegant the coding, or how smart your team of engineers.

The best product does not win. The best story wins.

The winner is not the engineer with the best MVP (minimum viable product). The winner is the leader with an alt-MVP (masterful visionary pitch).

A clear, concise, compelling message is like a magnet that attracts investors, clients, a five-star team, traction, and media coverage. Your business can take off.

You absolutely MUST have this message to build a thriving business. I call this kind of compelling message a "Million-Dollar Message." In Silicon Valley, it could potentially be a billion-dollar message. If you are running a small business, it could be a five or six-figure message. But I'll be referring to it as a Million-Dollar Message in this book.

Many of my clients are disrupters, such as Jason Henneberry, CEO, Tango Financial. When we started working together, he was running a six-figure startup with a small, loyal team of a dozen people. Still smarting from a prior business defeat, Jason was like a Phoenix rising from the ashes. He was on fire with great ideas, including a concept akin to becoming the Amazon.com of the Canadian mortgage industry.

Jason was frustrated that his breakthrough ideas had not yet produced the results that he knew that they could. He needed more cash and a bigger team to execute the projects that he saw so clearly in his mind's eye. He and his team took the Million-Dollar Message and Thought Leader and Media training to become more effective communicators.

Sometimes, I get discouraged running my business. Perhaps you can relate. On frustrating days, all the hours I put in don't seem worth it. But then I get a note from a client, and I remember my vision and my purpose. I'm reminded of how meaningful it is to me to be a catalyst for others to step into their greatness.

Getting this note from Jason Henneberry was like that. He wrote, "Aurora Winter and I crossed paths at a very interesting time in my career. My business evolved exponentially, and my team grew to more than 400 people. I appreciate the calm, cool approach Aurora brings to the table. I truly appreciate what Aurora has done for me and the rest of the team. She is a rock star, and I'm lucky to have her on my team!"

$10M RAISED

As we worked together, Jason refined his message and became much more powerful, poised, and polished. As a result, he was able to raise about $10 million in several rounds of financing.

In just two years, he's gone from running a six-figure company to running an eight-figure company.

Jason Henneberry is an extraordinary entrepreneur destined for greatness. I see him as Canada's young up-and-coming version of Sir Richard Branson.

LIFE-CHANGING CHOICES

In 1999, my then eleven-year-old son, Yale Winter, was obsessed with the idea of becoming a video game designer. A mutual friend introduced him to Tarrnie Williams, then a video game producer for Electronic Arts. Tarrnie generously took Yale under his wing and mentored him, giving my son a mountain of books on coding video games, and weekly homework assignments. As a result, Yale's skills flourished, he won a full-tuition scholarship, and is now a video game designer and software engineer. Tarrnie's mentoring changed the trajectory of Yale's life, and I'm deeply grateful.

Tarrnie's first mentor was his father, who launched Canada's first publicly traded software company, SDC, which grew from nil to $21M in five years. With decades of experience in the video game industry, Tarrnie has produced and shipped over a billion-dollars of video games.

When he worked at EA [Electronic Arts] in Los Angeles, Tarrnie worked insane hours, 100-hour workweeks. "I missed my son's second year because I was working so much. I distinctly remember one Saturday morning, I called a meeting so that we could get ahead of things. We were probably five months from finalizing the video game so that deadline was looming over our heads," Tarrnie said.

As the senior producer running a team of 170 people, only the Executive Producer and General Manager were above him structurally. To get ahead of things, Tarrnie called a meeting of the leadership team of 22 people on Saturday morning. Everyone showed up, including Tarrnie's two-year-old son.

Instead of appreciating the extra effort, the Executive Producer and General Manager rebuked Tarrnie for starting the meeting at 10 am instead of 9 am—on a Saturday!

It was a turning-point. Tarrnie quit and moved his family back to Vancouver, BC, Canada. He decided to start his own business and launched Blueprint Reality with co-founder Ben Sheftel. Blueprint Reality is disrupting the Augmented Reality (AR) and Virtual Reality (VR) space.

When we started working together in 2016, Tarrnie had a brand-new startup, no employees, no investors, and no traction. He was excited about his new venture and brought a lot of expertise to the table. Yet he was understandably concerned about his message as few people understood the potential of Virtual Reality. He needed a way to honestly yet powerfully reframe his pivot, and simultaneously position Blueprint Reality as a potential unicorn in the VR space.

His attention-grabbing message is, "Virtual Reality is the biggest change to hit humanity since fire. The myth is that VR is just for gamers. The fact is that exponential change means that VR will transform business. It will change the way we live, work, learn, and connect. Entire industries, including communication, education, entertainment, manufacturing, and medicine, will all be upended."

STARTUP LAUNCHED

Once he got clear on his message, he was able to close a deal with INTEL, raise several million dollars, and hire employees.

His team and I were thrilled. Tarrnie is the kind of extraordinary leader who inspires loyalty and devotion. When times were tough, his team stuck by him and continued working long hours even though there was no money, at that moment, to pay them. One of the ways he inspires loyalty is by generously acknowledging others.

For example, Tarrnie posted this recommendation on LinkedIn, "Aurora Winter is an incredible champion for startups and new technologies. She has been unwavering in her support of my new business as we've raised capital and gained traction. We're collaborating on a book titled, *Virtual Meets Reality: Forging Connections Between The Real and Virtual Worlds*. Today is an exciting time of exponential technological change. This book has benefited from Aurora's considerable research into tech trends, triggered years ago when her son became a game developer (and later became a software engineer in VR). If you're looking for someone to bolster your team with striking insights and boundless energy and passion, I highly recommend Aurora. She brings a fresh, thoughtful perspective to the table."

Blueprint Reality is positioned to become the standard SDK (software development kit) in the VR and AR industry. There is going to be a unicorn in this space, and I believe that Blueprint Reality is a contender. In other words, they could become the standard—like the Microsoft Windows of VR. Being the industry standard created a fortune for Bill Gates, and could potentially create a fortune for Blueprint Reality.

YOU CAN'T OUTSPEND A WEAK MESSAGE

To recap, a clear vision, coupled with a compelling message, is the highest-leverage and lowest-cost tool in your toolkit as an innovative entrepreneur. You can never outspend a weak message.

Your Million-Dollar Message is your secret weapon to multiply your success. It attracts the right people to work for you, buy from you, invest in you, partner with you.

Your Million-Dollar Message has the potential to:

- Raise millions from investors
- Generate millions in new business
- Reach millions of people through the media
- Increase your impact, income, and influence

Having a Million-Dollar Message is more important than ever before in our rapidly-changing economy. Exponential change means massive changes in the marketplace. There will be big winners and big losers.

People are hungry for leaders with vision. Your vision is the blueprint. As you read this book, make notes, and build your vision for the future.

Watch the video *Your Million-Dollar Message* to learn how you can create your own message. You can access this video and other bonuses here: www.ThoughtLeaderBonuses.com.

"Success isn't about how much money you make, it's about the difference you make in people's lives."
~ Michelle Obama ~

3 YOUR BRAND

"A brand for a company is like a reputation for a person. You earn reputation by trying to do hard things well."
~ Jeff Bezos ~

Let's look at the secret that Oprah Winfrey used to build a billion-dollar empire and become one of the most beloved Thought Leaders in the world. You can use this winning strategy in your business, too.

You Don't Own Your Most Valuable Asset

YOUR BRAND IS the key to commanding premium pricing. Your brand is the key asset you sell if you sell your company or your shares in your company. But you don't own your most valuable business asset: your brand.

Your brand lives in the mind of the marketplace. You don't own that mind. That mind has a very tiny amount of shelf space for you. So you need to have a clear, concise, compelling message.

For example: "We launch Thought Leaders." That's what my business does. Short and snappy.

If you don't have a brand, you are in a commodity business. You don't have a competitive advantage. That is a terrible strategy. Without a brand, your business is vulnerable to hungrier, smarter, faster, lower-cost providers like Walmart. You don't want to compete with Walmart. Or China. Or robotics and AI. You will lose.

A BRAND IS A STORY

What is a brand? Your brand is not a logo. It's a story. It's how other people perceive you, what they say about you.

Your brand is:

- The story of your customers
- The story of the problems you solve
- The story of the wow results that you create
- The origin story of launching your business
- The story of why you do what you do

Your brand is your mission, your reason why. Or, as author Simon Sinek put it, "People don't buy what you do, they buy why you do it."

Your brand is what you stand for. It's your promise, like Coca Cola's "It's the real thing" or Nike's "Just do it."

How Oprah Built a Billion-Dollar Brand

OPRAH WINFREY IS best known for her multi-award-winning talk show *The Oprah Winfrey Show*, which was nationally syndicated from 1986 to 2011. Heralded as the greatest black philanthropist in American history by *BusinessWeek*, Oprah is one of the most influential women in the world today.

Yet Oprah was not born with any advantages. Quite the contrary. She had a difficult, abusive, and impoverished childhood. In between her crushing childhood and her meteoric rise to super-stardom, she worked hard, studied hard, and prayed hard. And she did one more thing brilliantly.

Oprah cultivated and reinforced her brand. She did something bold and utterly unconventional—featuring her photo on the front cover of **every** issue of O Magazine. Unheard of! Brilliant!

Creating a strong brand is one of the reasons that Oprah is a billionaire. To see how you could model her example, watch the video *The Secret Oprah Used to Build a Billion-Dollar Empire*: www.ThoughtLeaderBonuses.com.

Unlike some celebrities, Oprah behaved the same way whether the cameras were rolling or not. My client, Dr. Tracy Thomas, wrote about her experience at Harper Studios in her book *The Method*. During the commercial breaks, Oprah grumbled that her Jimmy Choo shoes were a size too small. Dr. Tracy realized that the $3,000 pair of shoes were likely going to get tossed in a closet or donated to Goodwill.

Dr. Tracy wrote, "When the next commercial break came, and Oprah started to grumble again about the shoes, my hand spontaneously shot up in the air. I piped up, loud and clear, "I'll take them!" ... Oprah scanned the audience until she locked eyes with me. Shoes in hand, she started up the aisle to where I was sitting. She was saying, "No way these will fit you—you're petite, your feet will be too small." I insisted, "No, no—I'm a size nine, just like you," and I kicked my foot right up into the air, as if I were Cinderella.

"And Oprah, without batting an eye, held the shoe up to my foot like Prince Charming. Sure enough, it was a match. Placing the Jimmy Choo shoes into my eager arms, she said, "They're all yours." Over her shoulder, she told the audience, "You've got to ask for what you want in life." Of course, everyone started laughing and clapping, loving the spontaneous display of outrageous generosity that Oprah is known for."

Oprah was authentically her generous brand, and as a result, Dr. Tracy shared a story about Oprah. Now I've shared that story with you. That's a viral message and a great brand!

"We did it! You have another best-selling author that you've nurtured. This couldn't have happened without you," wrote Dr. Tracy when her book *The Method* was released. "*The Method* is infinitely better thanks to your input."

Your Brand Is Your Story

MANY BUSINESSES MISTAKENLY believe that they own their brand. Your brand is your story. It's the story people say about you—when you're **not** in the room.

Your brand lives in the mind of the marketplace. You don't own that mind. You can catch the heartstrings of the marketplace by being remarkable. But you cannot force people to think the way you want them to.

Here, I'll prove it to you. Think of Bill Cosby. See? He was once a beloved icon representing wholesome family values. He produced and starred in *The Cosby Show*, the top-rated show in America. When dozens of women accused him of rape and sexual assault, Cosby's honorable image shattered. In 2018, he was classified as a sexually violent predator and sentenced to prison.

His brand is destroyed. No matter how much he spends on advertising and PR spin, he will never be able to reclaim that pristine, wholesome brand. As a result, his once-magnetic brand is now toxic. His business and his brand have been flushed down the toilet.

Your company's brand value will be one of the most significant elements in the valuation of your company if you build a great brand and business. Brand value is sometimes called "goodwill" on the asset sheet. It is the difference between the value of the company's net assets (cash, buildings, inventory, accounts receivables) and the amount you can sell your company for.

BUILD YOUR BRAND

Think long term—never tarnish the value of your brand. Your brand is your most valuable business asset.

Build your brand with:

- Your book(s)
- Your Intellectual Property (IP)
- Copyright, patents, trademarks

- Your unique branded system (UBS)
- Your unique distribution system
- Your list / community / followers
- Your message—be bold, clear, concise, compelling
- Your video marketing funnel
- Your reputation
- Your TED talk
- Your media appearances

To build a valuable brand, be strategic—dominate a small marketplace, then expand. Don't try to be all things to all people (mediocracy). Be the very best at something specific (mastery).

BE YOUR BRAND

Your words whisper, your actions shout. What does your brand stand for? Be those qualities. Be the client you want to attract. Be congruent. That is integrity. Integrity is magnetic. It is the foundation of lasting success.

If you want clients who are decisive, resourceful, innovative, creative and committed, then be those qualities. Be decisive, resourceful, innovative, creative, and committed.

If you want clients who take massive action, get outstanding results, send you referrals, and become loyal fans singing your praises, then model those qualities. Take massive action, get exceptional results, send referrals generously, and appreciate your mentors (you could start by thanking your Mom).

PIVOTING

Pamela Robertson is passionate about family, faith, and Tiny Homes. Her vision is affordable housing for everyone so that people are not "house rich and cash poor." Her faith was tested again and again as she launched her brand-new business. Building Tiny Homes was unlike her prior business as a consultant. Her new business demanded a daunting amount of new skills, team members, and cash.

Pivoting is difficult, as you leave behind the certainty of what you know to venture into unknown territory. Entrepreneurs are very vulnerable during this transition, like a hermit crab that has outgrown its shell and risks being defenseless as it relocates into a bigger, better one. Entrepreneurs and hermit crabs alike cannot always choose safety or they will become stunted, trapped in a situation that is too confining. I've experienced this vulnerable, susceptible phase every time I've pivoted or launched a new business, so I have deep empathy for entrepreneurs in transition.

In spite of many seemingly-insurmountable obstacles, Pam kept the faith. She remained true to her family values. She hired her mother, her two sons, and her uncle. Pam remained committed to her vision of affordable housing for all. She walked through the fire of launching a startup and emerged on the other side with more faith, capabilities, and cash.

As a result, her company, Sunshine Tiny Homes Ltd., has attracted loyal clients with similar values. In under a year, Pam has successfully launched her new business, sold many Tiny Homes, and is well on her way to having a thriving multi-million-dollar business.

Pam was delighted to see her photograph featured on the front cover of the *Coast Life* magazine with the article "Big Love for Tiny Homes: Simpler Living on a Smaller Scale." She sent me the cover image with this text, "Thank you so much for the solid message and the courage! I am forever grateful, and the first person I always want to tell of my accomplishments is you!"

Her success is deeply meaningful to me. If you are a leader or mentor, I expect you can relate. It is so satisfying to contribute to the growth and success of others.

Words like hers immunize me from life's inevitable ups and downs and make me eager to get out of bed in the morning. Pamela Robertson's words warmed my heart.

Pam Robertson wrote, "When I first contacted Aurora, I had no idea what my startup company could become. I am so thankful that I connected with Aurora and enrolled in her Million-Dollar Message training. This program was invaluable, and it gave me the assistance I needed to get my company off the ground.

"Working with Aurora and connecting with the group of Thought Leaders has been the cornerstone of the greatness that my business is today! If it hadn't been for Aurora and her amazing coach Diane, I don't know where I would be. There was a time when I wanted to put it all down and walk away, but their insight and encouragement kept me going even when the going was tough. Taking the Thought Leader program has strengthened me as an individual, as a leader in my industry, and it has given me confidence that I never thought existed! I would recommend Aurora and her amazing training to anyone who wants to grow, excel, and take the lead in what they do."

A strong brand has coherent values. Here's an example of the core values of Zappos as Tony Hsieh shared in his book *Delivering Happiness*.

ZAPPOS: 10 CORE VALUES

1. Deliver WOW Through Service
2. Embrace & Drive Change
3. Create Fun & a Little Weirdness
4. Be Adventurous, Creative, and Open-Minded
5. Pursue Growth & Learning
6. Build Open, Honest Relationships with Communication
7. Build a Positive Team & Family Spirit
8. Do More with Less
9. Be Passionate & Determined
10. Be Humble

What are your insights about your brand? What are the core values of your brand? What is important?

Which of the above values from Zappos resonate with you? Does your brand seek to WOW and deliver something above and beyond what's expected? Do you embrace and drive change? Does your brand care about helping people grow and learn?

If so, one way you could demonstrate that you care about people is by sharing this book. It's easy and free. Just post on social media or send an email. To save you time, here's a suggestion of what you could write:

"I'm reading a book called *Thought Leader Launch* and thought it would interest you. You can get a free *Thought Leader Launch* starter library here: www.ThoughtLeaderLaunch.com. This book will help you build your business, your book, and your brand."

HOW TO BRAND ANYTHING

My brother, Bryce Winter, has always been interested in branding and design. As a blonde-haired boy of seven seated in the back seat of our family car, he could reliably identify the make and model of oncoming vehicles at night just by seeing their headlights. I can't even do that in broad daylight!

Bryce has thought deeply about branding archetypes. He shares his branding systems in his books, *Signs and Symbols of Success*, and *How to Brand Anything*.

To help you build your own brand, watch the bonus training video *The Secret Oprah Used to Build a Billion-Dollar Empire*. Get it here: www.ThoughtLeaderBonuses.com.

> *"Branding demands commitment; commitment to continual reinvention; striking chords with people to stir their emotions; and commitment to imagination. It is easy to be cynical about such things, much harder to be successful."*
>
> ~ Sir Richard Branson ~

4 YOUR SPOTLIGHT

"How do you judge the brightness of a light when you're the source? A spotlight can never see the shadows it casts."

~ Neal Shusterman ~

You're Not In The Business You Think You're In

YOU'RE NOT IN the business you think you're in—because (*drum roll, please*) —you're in show biz!

Thought Leaders need to showcase their big ideas and compelling vision. Entrepreneurs need to showcase their products and services.

Amateurs "wing it" and get unpredictable results. Professionals train and get reliable results. It is a skill to learn how to engage, enroll, and enthrall an audience. It is a skill to learn how to pitch your ideas and get the results you want. The bad news is that most people don't communicate effectively. The good news is that communication is a teachable skill.

YOU'RE IN SHOW BIZ!

Creating media buzz and attracting millions of dollars of free publicity is one of the reasons that Apple grew from a fledgling upstart to an industry leader.

Steve Jobs knew that he was in show business. Understanding the value of revealing the latest Apple product with showmanship, Jobs practiced and polished his presentation for weeks. What could have been a bland business announcement became a riveting two-hour must-watch commercial for Apple enthusiasts, triggering an avalanche of sales and media coverage.

To see how you could benefit from Steve Jobs' winning approach, watch the bonus video *How to Get Millions of Dollars of Free Publicity (even if you're not famous)* here: www.ThoughtLeaderBonuses.com.

"[Speaking is] the best way to make a lot of money in an hour—without a gun," according to Dan Kennedy, whose presentations have generated millions of dollars.

The right pitch can produce millions of dollars when delivered one-to-one. Imagine what it can do when broadcast one-to-many through the media!

Most entrepreneurs don't rehearse and practice—but the ones who do make the most money in sports, film, pitching, and business. Smart entrepreneurs understand that they're in show business and step into the spotlight. The right message and the right messenger can trigger media coverage. This can make the company rich and the CEO famous.

Instead of wasting money on advertising, they benefit from free media coverage. Instead of having an army of writers in their PR department, they profit from the best writers in the world writing about them—for free—and publishing stories in the top magazines. Instead of having the expense of their own TV studio, they hijack the equipment, talent, and audiences of top TV shows to showcase their products, services, and ideas.

The media needs news. Can you share something newsworthy? Do you have something interesting, entertaining, informative, or controversial to say? Do you have expertise or experience that can provide a fresh point-of-view on the topics currently in the news? Every DAY, media needs more than 10,000 guest experts in America alone. If you can turn your topic into an engaging show, you can get free air time.

You do not have to reach everyone on the planet to become recognized as a Thought Leader in your industry. Start with a narrow focus on what appeals to your target market.

Consider podcasts, YouTube channels, social media, public speaking, conferences, and other opportunities to share your message one-to-many. For example *The Joe Rogan Experience*, *The Tim Ferriss Show*, *Marie TV*, Oprah's *SuperSoul Sunday*, TEDx, TED, E3, A-Fest, SXSW, and other conventions, events, and awards specific to your industry such as *Top 40 Under 40*.

CELEBRITY CONNECTIONS

The world was shocked by the news that celebrity chef Anthony Bourdain took his own life on June 8, 2018. I mourned the loss of my friend. I had invited Bourdain into my home, and I got to know, like, and trust him over dinner. I don't invite strangers into my home to share a meal. Do you?

So, while Anthony Bordain did not know me, I knew him from watching his TV series *Parts Unknown*. He had earned a place in my heart.

That is the magic of watching someone on a screen. Video triggers our visual and auditory senses. Our brain makes neural connections as if we had met the person. Setting matters, so when we repeatedly invite someone into the privacy of our own home, our brain concludes that this person is a trusted friend or family member.

We do business with people we know, like, and trust. You don't need to be a globe-trotting celebrity chef with a TV show to build trust. But you don't have to meet everyone in person, either. Connections can be forged through books, audios, and videos. Make it easy for people come to know, like, and trust you.

The 64/4 Rule

SUCCESSFUL LEADERS SEEK to understand psychology and the laws of human nature. They study how to influence, inspire, and impact others. They leverage the Pareto principle (the 80/20 rule) to optimize the allocation of limited resources, including time and money.

The Pareto principle states that roughly 80% of the results come from just 20% of the inputs. For example, 20% of your customers will account for 80% of your sales. Or 20% of your time will generate 80% of your revenue.

Resources of time and money are limited, so it is essential to allocate resources in a manner that maximizes the payoff. Look for the high-leverage 20% of causes that will yield disproportionately large results.

Applying the 80/20 rule to the top 20% yields 4% (20% × 20% = 4%). In other words, 4% of activities will produce 64% of the results (80% × 80% = 64%). This is the 64/4 rule. It infers that allocating a trivial 4% of resources will produce more than half of the results (64%)! In my experience, communicating is in this highly-leveraged top 4%. Communication is a superpower.

To illustrate this with a hypothetical example, let us imagine that Steve Jobs worked 1000 hours every 20 weeks. Assuming the Pareto principle rule applied, a mere 40 hours of his time (4% of 1,000 hours) would produce a mammoth 64% of the total results. Steve Jobs practiced for three weeks to present the wildly-successful Apple launches. You do the math.

Smart leaders understand and leverage the neuroscience of communication.

Neuroscience

"HERE'S THE "BIG idea" in 76 words: There is a fundamental disconnect between the way we pitch anything and the way it is received by our audience. As a result, at the crucial moment, when it is most important to be convincing, nine out of ten times we are not. Our most important messages have a surprisingly low chance of getting through. You need to understand why this disconnect occurs in order to overcome it, succeed, and profit," wrote Oren Klaff in his excellent book *Pitch Anything*.

People make a big mistake when they believe the message they send is the message that's received. Smart people think if they send the equivalent of a verbal "Excel spreadsheet" to another intelligent person, that their message is going to be opened with

Excel. That's not what happens. Ideas are viruses. So the listener needs to do a "virus scan." But doing a virus scan is a bother, so first, the listener has to decide if your message is worth the effort—if the juice is worth the squeeze.

All this happens subconsciously in the flash of a few seconds, and it is based upon the way our brains evolved.

CROC BRAIN

Our reptilian brain, or "croc brain," evolved first. It is responsible for the initial filtering of messages. It has strong, primal emotions and is responsible for keeping us safe and alive. (The reptilian brain includes the brainstem and cerebellum, and is reliable but rigid and compulsive. It evolved 250 million years ago in reptiles.) You need to get past this ancient gatekeeper.

An easy way to remember this is to picture a castle with a moat around it. The moat is teeming with crocodiles. You're like a knight riding upon a snow-white horse with an urgent letter to deliver to the King and Queen residing inside this castle.

You need to get past this crocodile and get the drawbridge to come down, granting you access. First, you need to get attention. The croc brain is alert for danger. If you're too dangerous, the drawbridge will not come down. If you're too boring, obvious, or predictable, the drawbridge will not come down. You cannot be like every other messenger who has come by this week.

You need to trigger enough tension to attract attention. But not so much tension as to trigger fear. You need to entice the drawbridge to come down by showing that you have something interesting, new, worthwhile, valuable. The croc brain responds to primal messages: food, sex, danger. Like a crow, it likes shiny objects and baubles.

If you succeed, the drawbridge comes down, and you can prompt your horse to trot over it. You're now past the fortified outer walls. But you do not yet have an audience with the King and Queen. You have to face the next challenge: the mid-brain.

MID-BRAIN

In human evolution, the mid-brain was next to appear. Humans are not strong or fast. We do not have sharp claws or teeth. To survive as a species, we needed to band together. Alone, we perished. Together, we thrived.

The mid-brain remembers agreeable and disagreeable experiences from the past and makes value judgments about the meaning of social situations. (It evolved 150 million years ago in mammals, and includes the hippocampus, the amygdala, and the hypothalamus.)

Mounted on your horse, you trot into the courtyard, bearing your essential message for the King and Queen. Inside the courtyard are the garrison, stables, workshops, and homes of knights and nobility. You need to pass the social "sniff test" here before you are allowed to go to meet the King and Queen in the inner sanctum.

The social mid-brain is alert to status, power, and influence. It checks if you, as a knight, have enough status to see the King and Queen. Does your message have status—is it from another King or Queen? Who else thinks this message is important? Is this a Trojan horse—or can this message be trusted?

The social mid-brain rapidly assesses status, authority, trust. Gatekeepers have been specifically instructed not to send any message up to the King and Queen unless it is important, new, and exciting. If you fail this test, you will be ousted from the castle (and fed to the crocodiles). In ancient times, being outcast meant certain death.

If you pass this test, you will be granted a brief audience with the King and Queen. Luckily, you succeed, so a stable boy takes your horse, and you mount the stairs to the castle keep, flanked by knights who remain alert to your every move.

NEOCORTEX

The palace doors swing open. You are ushered into the throne room. The King and Queen have deigned to hear your message. But if you've watched *Game of Thrones*, you know that you cannot assume this audience will last long—or that it is without danger.

Finally, you can deliver your message to the King and Queen: the neocortex. This is the part of the brain that can understand your message and take action on it. The neocortex is where we process language, ideas, abstract thought, imagination, and innovation. (Our sophisticated problem-solving neocortex appeared about three million years ago in primates.)

If you maintain interest, you will be granted a more extended audience. If you drone on, you will be abruptly cut off (and fed to the crocodiles).

The neocortex is divided into a left brain and right brain, the King and Queen in this metaphor, which processes information differently. One side of the brain tends to be more linear and logical, the other side more holistic and creative. Every person, regardless of sex, has both hemispheres. When you're delivering your message, you will have the most success by addressing both hemispheres and maintaining the interest of both the King and the Queen.

Communication is a core skill for success today. As Chris Anderson, Head of TED wrote in *TED Talks*: "Presentation literacy isn't an optional extra for the few. It's a core skill for the twenty-first century. It's the most impactful way to share who you are and what you care about. If you can learn to do it, your self-confidence will flourish, and you may be amazed at the beneficial impact it can have on your life, however you might choose to define that."

People have been telling stories around the campfire for years. Today, show business, public speaking, and pitching capture our attention using story-telling, intrigue, prizing, revelation, human interest, surprise, reversals, and more.

A movie is an idea wrapped in emotion. So is a great pitch. People don't buy with logic. They buy with emotion. They buy stories. But first, they buy your vision.

Once you have your message, it is vital to practice under pressure. This produces a great message and a confident, polished messenger.

THE VALUE OF VIDEO

Videos create an intimate, personal connection. They nurture relationships and broadcast your expertise and humanity into the viewer's home. You're viewed as a celebrity, a star, a friend, and a trusted expert.

Shockingly, people remember videos even after a few seconds. Research published by Facebook demonstrated that people remember videos at a statistically significant rate after viewing only .25 seconds! Amazing! On Facebook, the average viewing time is 1.7 secs on mobile, 2.5 seconds on desktop. The right videos will reinforce your star status faster than anything else.

Fortunately, people linger much longer on YouTube, with the average viewing session being 40 minutes.

Here are a few statistics that underscore the value of video:

- 100 Million Hours of Video per DAY are watched on Facebook.—*Tech Crunch*
- People watch over a billion hours of YouTube videos every DAY.—*Brandwatch*
- The average viewing session on YouTube is more than 40 minutes.—*Brandwatch*
- 79% of all global consumer internet traffic will be video by 2018.—*Cisco*
- Social video generates 1200% more shares than text and image combined.—*Brightcove*
- Video ads have an average CTR of 1.84%, the highest click-through rate of all digital ad formats.—*Business Insider*
- TED talks were viewed 125 million times every month (2016).—*TED Talks*
- 96% of consumers find videos helpful when making purchase decisions.—*Animoto*

A video is only a delivery mechanism—you still need the right message.

My client Violet Lange helps successful, spiritual women thrive in life and in love. She nailed her message in our Million-Dollar message training. As part of her homework, Violet shot videos, using our fill-in-the-blank recipes. She then posted these videos on her own Facebook page and generated $45,000 of new business in less than two months. Violet was thrilled. Recently married, she wanted to take some time off to have a baby, and the extra cash gave her a cushion to do that.

Golden Spotlight

DRS. JUSTENE AND Janice Doan, DDS, stepped into the spotlight as authors, speakers, and experts when we published their book *Keys to a Healthy Smile After 40: 7 Secrets to Feeling 7 Years Younger.*

As a result of becoming published authors, the Doan sisters were greeted like celebrities by their most-accomplished peers. The organizers of the Incisal Edge *Top 40 Under 40* conference for dentists in New York bought copies of *Keys to a Healthy Smile After 40* to give to every attendee. Top dentists eagerly crowded around the new authors, asking, "Can I have your autograph?"

To give you a taste of their fantastic story (which was picked up by over 240 media outlets), here's one of the press releases we sent out to launch their book:

FROM CONCENTRATION CAMP TO THRIVING 7-FIGURE DENTAL PRACTICE

New Book by Top San Diego Dentists Dr. Justene Doan and Dr. Janice Doan.

For the first time, the Doan sisters publicly reveal their dramatic and miraculous story of going from a concentration camp with their only possessions being the threadbare clothes on their backs—to immigrating to America, learning English, getting an education, and eventually establishing a thriving seven-figure business, A+ Family Dentistry in San Diego.

The new book, *Keys to a Healthy Smile After 40* by Dr. Justene Doan and Dr. Janice Doan, shares both practical and profound ways to have a beautiful smile.

Recognized as "Top 40 Under 40" dentists in America in 2015, Dr. Justene Doan and Dr. Janice Doan have been featured in the media as exceptional dentists.

The Doan sisters understand dental care both personally and professionally. They both have beautiful, healthy white smiles today—but it wasn't always that way.

Janice and Justene were born in Vietnam. After the Vietnam war ended in 1975, their prospects were bleak. The girls tried to escape, but were captured and imprisoned in a concentration camp. They didn't have enough to eat—or even a toothbrush. Their teeth were full of cavities. Their book reveals the miraculous story of their harrowing escape from Vietnam to America.

After receiving dental care in the US and experiencing first-hand the transformation in their health, confidence, and smiles, the Doan sisters decided to become dentists. They now help others using their unique branded system of empathy, education, and the latest breakthrough techniques in dentistry.

As a child, Justene assumed that everyone would lose their teeth when they got older. Teeth were important and precious. Justene's grandmother, who was in her fifties, had dentures. Every morning in their kitchen in Vietnam, Justene watched as her grandmother would take out her dentures, brush them, and put them back in her mouth.

"I watched those dentures like a hawk. I wanted to make sure that I inherited that set of teeth," said Justene. "I would ask my grandma, "Grandma, when you pass away, can I have your teeth?"

Now a dentist, Dr. Justene Doan dedicates her life to helping others keep their teeth healthy for a lifetime. "Most people have no clue how to care for their teeth in their forties, fifties, and beyond. They're jeopardizing their smile and their health without knowing it. It's not their fault. No one has taken the time to explain what to do. My sister and I wrote *Keys to a Healthy Smile After 40: 7 Secrets to Feeling 7 Years Younger* to solve this problem."

"One of the secrets to feeling younger is—smile! Smiling helps you feel more confident and look younger. Your smile is the sexiest curve on your body!" said Dr. Janice Doan.

"Even when you're having a bad day, if you smile, your day will turn around. Not only does your smile communicate how you're feeling—it affects how you are feeling," said Dr. Justene Doan.

Publisher Aurora Winter said, "The authors' experience being in a concentration camp in the aftermath of the Vietnam war gave them a rare perspective on what matters. They're two of the most positive people I know. Their "rags to riches" story of triumphing over adversity would make a dramatic movie, and makes a fascinating read."

In the next chapter, I'll reveal how they wrote their book while tripling the size of their business—even though English is not their native language.

"People have been telling stories around the campfire for years. Today, videos, books, and movies capture our attention using story-telling, intrigue, prizing, revelation, human interest, reversals, and more. Today, the most successful leaders are story-tellers."

~ Aurora Winter ~

5 YOUR BUSINESS

"The first job of a leader—at work or at home—is to inspire trust. It's to bring out the best in people by entrusting them with meaningful stewardships, and to create an environment in which high-trust interaction inspires creativity and possibility."

~ STEPHEN COVEY ~

WE'RE CONTINUING TO explore what it takes to launch as a Thought Leader—even if you don't have connections or wealth. Here's a quick recap of what we've covered so far:

Your Million-Dollar Message

A clear vision, coupled with a compelling message, is the highest-leverage and lowest-cost tool in your toolkit as an leader or entrepreneur. A determined leader who has mastered the right Million-Dollar Message is practically unstoppable. The right message can trigger millions of dollars in capital for a startup. It can go viral, rapidly reaching over a million people, as we saw with my client's TEDx talk. A Million-Dollar Message can lead to a multi-million-dollar payday, as we saw with Arianna Huffington. Or put shoes on the feet of 95 million underprivileged children, as we saw with TOMS Shoes.

Your Brand

Your brand is not a logo. Your brand is a story—the story that other people tell about you (when you're not in the room). Without a brand, you're in a commodity business—which means you'll be competing on price alone. Good luck competing with Walmart, Target, and China! To avoid wafer-thin (or negative) profits, be clear what your brand stands for. Be congruent, not bashful—like Oprah. Over-deliver—like Zappos. Think big—like Elon Musk.

Your Spotlight

No matter what business you're in, you're in show business! You are in the business of showcasing your business. Think Hollywood meets Silicon Valley. The most persuasive presenters can win venture capital, premium clients, a superstar team, and our hearts (and wallets). Steve Jobs, Howard Schultz, and Sir Richard Branson are all masters at showcasing what they're doing in a way that attracts media coverage worth of millions of dollars.

Your Business

The speed of change is increasing, which makes people uncertain and uneasy. As a result, trust is more important than ever. In this chapter, we will look at how business moves at the speed of trust. Lack of trust stops growth. What's the best thing to do about that?

Crossing the Chasm

BUILDING A TRUSTED brand requires understanding consumer psychology. Markets are not homogeneous.

As Geoffrey Moore explained in his insightful book *Crossing the Chasm*, different markets respond differently to a new product or service. The adoption of a new product or service follows a normal distribution curve.

Behavior	%Market	Persuaded by
Innovators	2.5%	Self-motivated, inventors
Early Adopters	13.5%	Listen to the Innovators
	CHASM	
Early Majority	34%	Trust Early Majority Only
Late Majority	34%	Reluctant, needs early adoption
Laggards	16%	Only change when no option

The problem is that there's a chasm between the Early Adopters and the Early Majority.

The Early Adopters listen to the Innovators. Early Adopters are highly motivated. They seek a quantum leap forward. They're eager for something that was never before possible. They value the advantage of being first.

A new product or service can reach a mere 16% of the potential market without crossing the chasm. For a new business to take off and make money, it must cross the chasm.

But there's a big problem. The problem is that the Early Majority are not interested in the recommendations of the Early Adopters or the Innovators. The Early Majority distrust change. They want evolution, not revolution. They want to enhance, not overthrow, the status quo. They're willing to try something new when others like them—in the Early Majority—recommend it. That's a catch-22. Without a bridge to cross this chasm, many startups fail.

A book acts as a bridge between markets. The Early Majority are influenced by their trusted media sources (as well as the opinions of their like-minded friends).

Books are a trusted way that ideas go from being espoused by Innovators or Early Adopters to become embraced by the Early Majority, followed by acceptance by the Late Majority. A book unlocks valuable media coverage and helps ideas spill over from smaller, more innovative market segments to more considerable, more conservative, and more lucrative market segments. Becoming a media-savvy published author allows you to create a tipping point.

Many innovative startups attempt to force their way across the chasm by spending massive amounts on advertising. Facebook, Google, and other online ad platforms are glad to take their money. Some report that up to 40% of the funds invested by Venture Capital firms are spent on advertising to buttress a make-shift bridge across this chasm. But when the advertising stops, this bridge collapses.

The best way to cross the chasm is to get in a hot air balloon and float easily over it, landing gently in the lucrative green fields of the Early Majority. From there, the Late Majority can be annexed.

That hot air balloon is literally filled with hot air—yours. As an author and expert, you can share your views on respected podcasts and broadcasts. That way, you can build a trusted brand and get your message out to the masses.

Super Credibility

PETER DIAMANDIS HAS bold science-fiction ideas some might consider crazy, such as private spaceflight and mining asteroids for precious metals.

"To start this kind of company with any real hope of success and—equally difficult—to present it to the public in a plausible fashion requires a different kind of approach.... none more important than birthing projects above the line of super-credibility," wrote Diamandis and Steven Kotler in *Bold*.

They go on to explain that if you hear about a new idea **below** the line of credibility, you dismiss it. On the other hand, if you hear about a new idea **above** the line of credibility, you consider it. Best of all, when a new idea is broadcast above the line of **super-credibility**, you don't doubt it.

When Diamandis announced the X Prize for $10 million, he had a big, bold vision, but he did not have the $10 million. So he went to a great deal of effort to announce the X Prize above the line of super-credibility. Diamandis obtained the backing of billionaire investors (including Larry Page, Ross Perot, and Richard Branson), as well as the world's top space engineers (including Chris Lewicki, who had run three different billion-dollar Mars missions for NASA).

The X Prize promised $10,000,000 for the first non-government organization to "build and launch a spacecraft capable of carrying three people to 100 kilometers above the Earth's surface, twice within two weeks." The announcement triggered worldwide competition rather than skepticism.

Renamed the Ansari X Prize after the Ansari brothers donated several million, Diamandis delivered the $10,000,000 prize and launched a brand-new $2 billion private space industry, changing the course of history.

The winning team's technology was licensed by Richard Branson to create Virgin Atlantic.

MOORE'S LAW

In case you are not familiar with Moore's law, let me briefly touch upon it. It is important to understand what is driving exponential technological advancements. Gordon Moore, the founder of Intel, noticed that the number of integrated circuits on a transistor had been doubling every 12 to 24 months. That was sixty years ago, and in the intervening decades, there has been relentless progress in price and performance.

The result is that the smartphone in your pocket is a million times cheaper and a thousand times more powerful than a supercomputer from the 1970s. The applications in smartphones today would have been worth almost a million dollars if purchased separately just a short time ago. (Smartphone applications typically include GPS, camera, video conferencing, audio recorder, calendar, radio, library, and more.) Massive economic, social, and technological change were facilitated by Moore's law.

The network effect is another exponential example. Two hundred people using Uber doesn't impact the taxi industry, but thousands of people using Uber can devastate it. Thousands of people using Airbnb can upend the hotel industry. Other laws, based on similar principles, expand exponential implications in other fields.

The New Transformation Economy

IF MORE INFORMATION was the answer, everyone would be rich and thin. The information economy is dead. Long live the Transformation Economy!

People are hungry for transformation. They want experiences, connection, significance, meaning, and purpose. They want to transform everything from their bodies to their bank accounts.

The masters in this new economy will embrace change, dance with change, exploit change. They will be change agents. Companies want to stay on the leading edge, which means embracing and exploiting new opportunities without sabotaging employee morale, profits, or company culture. That's a tricky balancing act for the leadership team.

Entire industries are being disrupted by exponential technological change. There are billion-dollar opportunities to solve problems that impact entire markets, such as medicine, travel, entertainment, health care, education, and more. I've dubbed this new phase the Transformation Economy. To learn more, watch the video *The #1 Change in Our Economy*: www.ThoughtLeaderBonuses.com

WARNING: IGNORE MOORE'S LAW AT YOUR PERIL

Businesses that do not embrace change will be destroyed by it. For example, in 1955, the average life span of a Fortune 500 company was 75 years. That's a lifetime. But by 2015, the average life span of a Fortune 500 company had shrunk to 15 years. That's not even one generation. In the last 15 years, 52% of Fortune 500 companies have disappeared.

Now is a risky time for large, stagnant innovation-resistant companies. Kodak serves as a cautionary tale. Kodak invented the camera and then cornered the market on film. Next, Kodak invented the digital camera, but rejected it, certain no one would want such low-resolution photos. And besides, they were focused on selling Kodak film. Due to Moore's Law, those grainy digital images quickly became sharper and sharper. Everyone snaps digital photos now. And no one buys Kodak film.

End of story for Kodak. But it is just the beginning of the story for entrepreneurs exploiting Moore's Law.

FROM STARTUP TO $1 BILLION IN 2 YEARS

Massive new opportunities are opening up for small, nimble, entrepreneurial companies. For example, Amazon, Facebook, Uber, Lyft, Airbnb, eBay, Paypal, Priceline, DropBox, Skype, Calm, Thumbtack, to name a few. Disruptive new businesses are now feasible due to exponential progress in dozens of areas, including Augmented Reality (AR), Virtual Reality (VR), Artificial Intelligence (AI), 3-D printing, nanotechnology, robotics, biotech and more.

Instagram is an excellent example of an exponential opportunity seized by two young entrepreneurs. In October of 2010, Kevin Systrom and Mike Krieger founded Instagram. Sixteen months later, Instagram was valued at $25 million.

Instagram for Android was released in April 2012 and was downloaded more than a million times in just one day. Instagram was growing exponentially, with nearly 30 million users, even though it had only thirteen employees.

Less than two years after it was founded, **Instagram was bought by Facebook for $1 billion**—not a bad payday for Systrom and Krieger.

"If people like you, they will listen to you, but if they trust you, they'll do business with you."
~ ZIG ZIGLAR ~

6

YOUR MILLION-DOLLAR BOOK

"Almost anyone can be an author; the business is to collect money and fame from this state of being."
~ A. A. MILNE ~

BECOMING A MEDIA-SAVVY author and promoter could potentially launch a **billion**-dollar brand, as Sir Richard Branson, Arianna Huffington, and Howard Schultz have demonstrated. On the other hand, if you are a solopreneur, your book could potentially generate five or six figures—without selling any books.

But let's stick with a million-dollar outcome. We'll explore seven business strategies:

1. Attract Premium Clients & Premium Prices
2. Attract Investors, Launch Startup
3. Movie or TV Deal
4. Free Book & Upsell
5. Speaking
6. Training
7. Evergreen Bestseller

For clarity, we will look at each one as a stand-alone model. In reality, these models overlap. To succeed, focus. Decide which of these models is the best fit for your book, brand, and business, then tailor your approach like a glove to fit that model perfectly.

Over time, you'll most likely combine multiple models, as success in any one area will spill over to other areas. For example, Brené Brown's book triggered paid public speaking, then a TED talk. Next, Brown attracted media interviews, including Oprah's Super Soul Sunday, and in 2019 Brown has a special on Netflix, where she addresses a sold-out crowd as if she were a star standup comedian—rather than a "scientist story-teller."

But if Oprah hasn't interviewed you yet—focus! My personal favorite is the evergreen bestseller, which I've saved for last.

And if this is all beginning to sound like too much work, don't worry, I'll also walk you through some ways to delegate creating, publishing and promoting your book, as well as some ways to accelerate becoming a more powerful, polished presenter.

YOUR BEST STRATEGY IS NOT ...

Just in case you impatiently flipped ahead to this section of the book, let me reiterate: selling books fails to use the leverage a book represents. Your book is a "little hinge" that swings open big doors.

If you are banking on only selling books to make a million dollars, I urge you to get more creative, resourceful, and thoughtful with your business plan. I recommend that you consider the revenue from book sales as bonus money and leverage one of the seven recommended strategies that I'll be covering in a minute. Selling books is the slowest, hardest, and least-likely way to make a million dollars with your book.

For example:

- 50,000 books @ $20 each (self-published) = $1,000,000
- 1,000,000 books @ $1 royalty each (archaic publishing model) = $1,000,000

As you know by now, I don't recommend focusing your efforts on selling a book published by a large New York publisher, as the royalties will typically be around a dollar. So you would need to sell about a million books to generate a million dollars. A hybrid publishing model for international sales can be worthwhile, and I'll cover that later (in the Evergreen Bestseller section).

In every industry, including publishing, the role of the middleman is being eliminated. In his book, *Choose Yourself*, best-selling self-published author James Altucher wrote, "You no longer have to wait for the gods of corporate America, or universities, or investors, to come down from the clouds and choose you for success."

In his memoir, *I Can See Clearly Now*, Dr. Wayne W. Dyer wrote about his frustrating experience publishing his first book (*Your Erroneous Zones*) with a major publishing house. Dyer wrote, "I feel that *Your Erroneous Zones* will basically die on the vine before it is ever given the opportunity to ripen. I become a gigantic nuisance to all the powers that be at my publisher's headquarters. I talk to the publicity people, and they say that there is no budget allowance for the promotion of my book. I talk to the people at marketing, and they tell me there is no marketing plan for my book. I make calls to the people responsible for distributing my book to the bookstores, and no one returns my calls. Everything feels as if it is at a standstill."

Wayne Dyer refused to let his book be stillborn, so he started a bookstore and bought up the remainder of the first printing. When the first printing sold out, the publisher was forced to do a second printing. With 4,000 books in his bookstore (garage), he then bought out the entire second printing (about 2,500 books) to keep his book in print. With 6,500 books in his garage, he needed to sell them.

At his own expense, Dyer launched his own full-court-press marketing campaign. With his books in the trunk of his car and his wife and daughter accompanying him, he traveled across the country from radio station to radio station.

Dyer wrote, "It is normal for me to stay in a city for several days and do 12 to 14 interviews a day—often staying up all night doing late-night call-in radio.... The more interviews I do, the more the word begins to spread that I can do compelling interviews."

To recap, to overcome the frustrations of dealing with his publisher, Dyer started his own bookstore, devised his own marketing plan, did the distribution and delivery, and paid for his expenses as he marketed his book across the country. As a result of his efforts, *Your Erroneous Zones* eventually sold 35 million copies.

Today, it is much easier to cut out the middleman. You can promote your book and keep all the revenue rather than a tiny royalty. James Altucher, Seth Godin, Jeff Walker, and many other best-selling self-published authors have profited from cutting out the middleman, and you can, too.

Next, we will look at seven strategies to monetize your message, starting with looking at the value of attracting your ideal clients, people who place a premium value on the products and services you provide.

1. Attract Premium Clients & Premium Prices

BUSINESS MOVES AT the speed of trust. Your book creates trust. It enhances your expert status, creates a celebrity halo, and communicates your core values. A book creates an intimate connection.

Your book positions your business as the only logical choice for your ideal client. A book attracts affluent clients seeking the best solution, rather than bargain-hunters seeking the lowest price.

INCREASED TRUST, INCREASED SALES

Tony Robbins uses his books to keep his celebrity star shining brightly and attract people to his live events. He steps into the spotlight with media appearances, TED talks, and more. His books include *Unlimited Power*, *Awaken the Giant Within*, and *Money Master the Game*. Robbins is the founder of several companies with approximately $6 billion in annual sales.

Let's explore a hypothetical business that generates $50 million per year, with a Celebrity CEO at the helm—imagine someone like Tony Robbins. This CEO makes it easier for the sales team to enroll prospects and sell premium products and services (rather than the entry-level products and services).

What would be the result of a slight edge in sales? What would happen if the business stopped discounting? Improving the closing ratio by just 10% and enhancing the price by a mere 10% translates into an additional annual revenue of **ten million dollars!**

A slight edge makes a giant difference to the bottom line, as you can see in this example:

EXAMPLE #1:

- $50 million dollar per year business
- Increase close ratio by 10%
- Increase prices by 10%
- $50M × 1.1 × 1.1 = $60.05 million per year = an extra $10M per year

OVER THE NEXT 10 YEARS:

- × 10 years × $10M more per year = $100M more revenue (in 10 years)
- **Additional** value of business at exit or stock sale @ 2× earnings = 2 × $10M = $20M more share value (conservatively)
- TOTAL INCREASE IN VALUE = $120 million more

The real value does not end with the additional $10 million of revenue in a year. Over the next ten years, that is $100 million of extra income (ignoring compounding to keep things simple). The value of the company also increases. The company could easily be worth an **additional** $20 million or more when sold (using a benchmark multiple of 2× earnings). **This slight edge translates into an additional $120 million over 10 years!**

This winning strategy has been used by Sir Richard Branson, Tony Robbins, Arianna Huffington, and many others with thriving brands and businesses.

ATTRACT IDEAL CLIENTS

For an entrepreneur, a book is a great way to connect intimately with your tribe, share your vision, and become positioned as the only logical choice in your marketplace. It is a fantastic way to grow market share and leap-frog over much larger companies.

When we met, the Doan sisters were outstanding dentists, yet they were competing head-to-head with other dentists in San Diego, California. They had no way to set themselves apart in a competitive marketplace. They attracted new patients by slashing prices and giving free consultations—which did not position their business as a premium brand. Their online ads attracted a random cross-section of patients, and their "free exam" offers appealed to bargain-hunters.

Yet their business could serve patients seeking the best—rather than the cheapest. Dr. Justene Doan, DDS, was highly skilled in implant dentistry, had placed hundreds of implants, and had taken extensive postgraduate training. Her empathetic sister, Janice Doan, DDS, had a smile that lights up a room. Their marketing was not capitalizing on the fact that they're a phenomenal team providing the finest dental care.

As part of our *Thought Leader Book Launch* program, Dr. Justene and Dr. Janice realized that their ideal patient was over 40 years old. A patient in her 40s or 50s might need extensive dental work and could spend $5,000, $10,000, or even $20,000—10× as much as younger patients. The best business strategy for the Doan sisters was a book that attracted their ideal patient, positioned them as experts, and created their media platform. We agreed on this approach for their book.

Next, I interviewed them for two days, then my team and I polished their words and published their book *Keys to a Healthy Smile After 40: 7 Secrets to Feeling 7 Years Younger.*

The Doan sisters have done a phenomenal job growing their business from $1.5 million to $3 million. They are now opening a third office and are on track to generate $6 million. It's not surprising that other dentists are seeking them out for training and mentoring.

Growing their business from $1.5 million to $6 million in just a couple of years is a phenomenal result. Getting clear on their message, writing a book, and appearing on media certainly were contributing factors.

Their success leveraging their book, authority, and platform inspired this next example. Let's look at a hypothetical dental office that is attracting new patients with discount coupons and "free exam" offers, which do not attract the affluent. Many patients invest $400, rather than the $4,000 to $20,000 that an ideal patient would invest.

After writing and promoting a book designed to attract their ideal patient, this dental practice could serve more of their ideal patients at $8,000, rather than typical patients at only $400 each. That's a 20× increase. That means that if this dental office exclusively catered to their ideal patient, their revenue could increase by a factor of 20.

Let's be conservative and assume they only 2× the average value per patient overall. Most dental practices have excess capacity and empty chairs, so we will assume costs remain constant to keep this example simple.

Attracting more of their lucrative ideal clients so that they double their average transaction translates into an additional $1.5 million revenue per year for this dental practice. That's an additional $15 million over 10 years. The resale value of the dental practice, if sold, would increase by an estimated $3 million. The overall additional value is $18 million.

That means that the right book could be worth $18 million to this business—without a single copy of the book being sold!

EXAMPLE #2 (DENTAL PRACTICE):

- $1.5 million dollar per year business
- Double average transaction by attracting ideal patients
- $1.5M × 2 = $3 million per year = an extra $1,500,000 per year

OVER THE NEXT 10 YEARS:

- × 10 years × $1.5 million more per year = $15 million more revenue per decade
- **Additional** value of business at exit ÷ sale @ 2× earnings = 2 × $1,500,000 = $3,000,000 more share value (conservatively)
- TOTAL INCREASE IN VALUE = $18 million

A book can substantially increase revenue for doctors, dentists, and other professionals. In *Book the Business*, Dan Kennedy shared the result of a split test for health clinics, where a free book plus free exam offer was tested against just a free exam offer.

Kennedy reported, "Eighty percent of the prospective patients who came via the book offer enrolled in the doctors' programs versus 60 percent of those who enrolled in the free exam offer, and the average six-month dollar value of the book-offer patients was nearly double that of the other."

STAND OUT WHEN ADVERTISING IS REGULATED

A book is especially valuable in industries where advertising is tightly regulated, such as financial planning. For example, one financial planner wrote a book designed to appeal to newly-divorced, high-net-worth women (over $10 million). The financial planner dropped 50 copies of the beautiful book off at the offices of divorce attorneys in his area. This was gratefully received by the lawyers, as it added value for their clients. The new divorcees were eager for trusted advice, and the book made the author the trusted advisor, making him the only logical choice. As a result, the financial planner's business boomed.

Chiropractors have purchased my books by the case to give to their patients, knowing that the emotional and spiritual support provided by reading *From Heartbreak to Happiness* or *Grief Relief in 30 Minutes* would complement their treatments of the physical symptoms of grief and stress.

A book is an inexpensive yet meaningful way for a professional to be empathetic and provide additional support without taking any additional time. A gift book increases satisfaction, enhancing referrals, and loyal, repeat clientele.

YOUR BUSINESS CARD

People throw away business cards and brochures, but they value books and keep them for years. Your clients will pass on or recommend your books to their friends, making referrals easy. Your book can be your best business card. Books are widely available on Amazon, so they extend your reach nationally and internationally. Here are a few examples of using a book as a lead magnet:

- 100 new students at $10,000 each = $1,000,000
- 10,000 new students at $1,000 each = $1,000,000
- 1,000 new clients at $100,000 each = $100,000,000

Strategic Coach® is a flourishing 8-figure company, with revenues of approximately $30 million per year. The co-founder, Dan Sullivan, uses small books, which he typically publishes once a quarter, to increase engagement and add value. He has published more than 30 books, which attract clients who invest $25,000 to $100,000 per annum, with many clients staying for many years.

Sullivan's books become the basis of his radio and podcast interviews, increasing his media reach. If his books attract 100 new clients at $100,000 each, that translates into $10,000,000. If his books attract 1,000 new clients at $100,000 each, that translates into $100,000,000 of new revenue.

2. Attract Investors, Launch Startup

A BOOK CAN trigger investment in a startup. For example:

- 20 investors at $50,000 each = $1,000,000
- 3 investors at $2M each = $6,000,000
- Invest $1,000 × 1,000 clients = $1,000,000

As mentioned earlier, Jason Calacanis's book *Angel: How to Invest in Technology Startups—Timeless Advice from an Angel Investor Who Turned $100,000 into $100,000,000* attracted early-stage investment opportunities. Calacanis has invested in 74 companies, including Thumbtack, Calm, Tumblr, and Uber. So a book can attract investors—or be used by an investor to attract investment opportunities.

Calacanis runs an investment syndicate, which provides the opportunity for everyday people to invest smaller amounts in a startup. Here's what Calacanis wrote in 2017, "For close to 100 years non-accredited investors — currently defined as those making less than $200,000 a year or with less than one million in net worth excluding their home — have not been able to invest in private companies. That all changed this past May when the SEC started allowing everyone in the United States access to what I believe is the greatest wealth creation vehicle in the world today: startups. Over the past 10 years, startups like Dropbox, Mint (sold to Intuit for $170m), Yammer (sold to Microsoft for $1.2b), Fitbit (went public in June 2015), PowerSet (sold to Microsoft for $100m), Clicker (sold to CNET for $100m), Trello (sold to Atlassian for $425m), TrueCar (raised $70m in its 2014 IPO), and Cafe X (raised $5m) have presented at our event — but 97% of the people at the event were not allowed to invest in them. That has all changed."

I attended Calacanis's Launch event in San Francisco in the fall of 2018, which attracted 1,500 founders—so Calacanis gets a steady flow of new investment opportunities. His podcast *This Week In Startups* and *Angel: The Podcast* reinforces his status as a Thought Leader.

James Altucher built Stockpickr.com for less than $5,000 and sold it a few months later for $10 million. He has given away more than 100,000 copies of his books, on top of book sales, because he appreciates the long-term value of relationships. In *Choose Yourself*, he shared, "When I give away a book for free, it gets my name out there. That has a lifetime value for me that goes way beyond the few dollars I could maybe charge. When you add value to people's lives (for instance, giving away quality content for free), the opportunities that come back to you cannot be quantified."

3. TV or Movie Deal

A FILM OR TV deal can be lucrative. For example:

- TV or Film rights $1,000,000
- Ongoing royalties, syndication $1,000,000

When I worked as the head of development at Canada's largest film and television production and distribution company (then Atlantis Films), it was common to option the rights to a book and then set up a movie or TV series. The option amount was typically five or six figures, but the real money would flow once the TV series was broadcast, or the feature film opened in movie theaters. Successful movies and TV series can have a very long tail.

For example, Jennifer Aniston and her costars from the hit TV series *Friends* each received $1,000,000 per episode for the final season in 2004. According to a 2018 article in the *USA Today*, each star still earns $20,000,000 per year each from the syndication rights. That's right—$20M each. *Friends* generates a billion dollars a year for Warner Brothers. The creators, Kaufman and Krane, each have an estimated net worth of $400 million.

As an aside, I once got stuck in a middle seat on a flight from Vancouver, BC to Los Angeles. I was flanked by *Friends* star Matt LeBlanc and his friend, who had been skiing Whistler. That was about the only time I didn't mind sitting in the middle seat!

One of my clients, Timothy Forner, is writing a charming series of books about a dog detective. The first book is *Montgomery Schnauzer P.I & The Case of the Stealthy Cat Burglar*. His books would make a fantastic TV series or feature film. Pick up a copy for your kids or grandkids.

The appreciation is mutual: Tim posted this comment on my LinkedIn: "Aurora is a fantastic mentor and coach, as well as an expert in marketing. I highly recommend her help to refine your message and beam it to the world."

BIOPIC

Katharine Graham's memoir, *Personal History*, is the captivating inside story of the woman who ran the Washington Post during one of the most turbulent periods in the history of American media.

Her book captured the attention of screenwriter Liz Hannah, who said, "I read Graham's memoir, *Personal History*, and I absolutely fell in love with her." Hannah championed the idea of making a biographical drama. As a result, Steven Spielberg directed *The Post*, the true story of Kay Graham, starring Meryl Streep and Tom Hanks, which was nominated for two Academy Awards.

The Social Network (2010) is another biographical drama (or "biopic" as we say in the biz). The screenplay by Aaron Sorkin was adapted from Ben Mezrich's book *The Accidental Billionaires: The Founding of Facebook, a Tale of Sex, Money, Genius, and Betrayal*.

Ashton Kutcher portrayed Steve Jobs in the biographical drama "Jobs" (2013). It's the story of Steve Jobs' ascension from college dropout to one of the most revered creative entrepreneurs of the 20th century.

In my (admittedly biased) opinion, my book *From Heartbreak to Happiness: An Intimate Diary of Healing* would make a great film, along the lines of *Ghost* or *Truly Madly Deeply*.

REALITY TV

Marie Kondo's book *The Life-Changing Magic of Tidying Up: The Japanese Art of Decluttering* triggered a reality-TV series on Netflix. This TV series is especially surprising as Marie Kondo usually speaks in Japanese, so English subtitles frequently appear, which is practically unheard-of in a TV series produced for a North American audience. That underscores the power of a best-selling book. *The Life-Changing Magic of Tidying Up* has sold over 7 million copies worldwide and has been published in more than 40 languages.

Marie has succeeded in launching a movement that encourages people to cherish the things that "spark joy." Her philosophy of simplicity and gratitude goes far beyond the typical approaches to getting organized. Marie's mission is to "Organize the World." She has recently launched a KonMari Consultant training program (another revenue stream).

FUND-RAISER

Wayne Dyer supported PBS by using his books as gifts as "thank you" gifts for people who donated to PBS. Many people don't know that Dyer paid for the production of the first PBS specials, which helped make Dyer famous.

My friend Brahm Wenger used his children's books to create a TV show on PBS and Netflix called *Mack and Moxy*. Each episode showcased a celebrity and a charity. Advertising revenue, books, and DVDs were given to charities, including Habitat for Humanity, the World Wildlife Fund, and the America Heart Association. His work granted him an audience with President Obama and Michelle Obama in the White House.

4. Free Book & Upsell

THIS BUSINESS MODEL has become quite popular recently. Brendon Burchard, Dean Graziosi, Jeff Walker, and I have all used this model. Here's how you can make a million dollars with a free book plus upsell.

UPSELL

- Upsell $100 item (10,000 × $100 = $1,000,000)
- Upsell $2,000 product (500 × $2,000 = $1,000,000)

Let's look at Jeff Walker's experience using this model with his book *Launch*. Walker shared this information on the Genius Network podcast hosted by Joe Polish.

Walker gave away 40,000 books (by sending emails himself and through joint-venture (JV) partners). The book itself was free, but people paid $7 for shipping and handling (s&h). I estimate that $7 would cover Walker's out-of-pocket costs for printing and postage.

After people got the free book and paid for the shipping, Walker offered two upsells, one immediately for $197, and one after adding more value with a sequence of videos, for $1,997. Seven percent bought the $197 upsell, and 1.7% bought the $1,997 upsell, according to Walker.

Here's how he summarized the launch:

- $7 Free book & $7 s&h
- $14 7% upsell to $197 product (1 click upsell)
- $21 revenue per "free" book
- $34 1.7% upsell to $1,997 offer
- $55 revenue per book (on average)
- 41,000 books given away
- $2,255,000 revenue

Jeff Walker's example demonstrates that you can make 7 figures by giving books away for free! The average revenue per book is $55—more than the full retail price of a hardcover book. Even if Walker shared fifty percent of his income with his Joint Venture (JV) partners, he would still keep over a million dollars.

THE NEW YORK TIMES BESTSELLER LIST

The New York Times frowns upon this approach, it appears. In spite of having the numbers to qualify for *The New York Times* Bestseller list, Jeff Walker's book was ignored. (Typically, selling 10,000 books in the first week will result in making *The New York Times* bestseller list, and selling 3,000 books will make *The Wall Street Journal's* bestseller list.) Walker was not to be denied; he sold even more books, and the New York Times finally acknowledged *Launch* as a best-seller.

"The Times Best-Seller List: Another Reason Americans Don't Trust the Media," wrote Dennis Prager in an article published in *National Review*. Prager complained that his book published in

2018, *The Rational Bible*, did not make the list although it had outsold 14 of the 15 books on the list.

Jordan Peterson's 2018 book, *12 Rules for Life*, did not make *The New York Times* list either, in spite of selling 90,000 copies in the first two weeks, according to *Publisher's Weekly*. *The Exorcist* author sued *The New York Times* for not including his follow-up book on the list, and Deepak Chopra and others have apparently also threatened to sue *The New York Times* for the same reason.

Respected author Seth Godin said *The New York Times* bestseller list is "rigged." Reid Tracy, CEO of Hay House Publishing, urged authors to focus on writing an excellent book instead of getting distracted with bestseller lists. I agree.

Having your book on a bestseller list provides bragging rights, but it reflects just one week of book sales. Rather than focus on spiking sales for one week, I recommend that you build an evergreen bestseller that adds value to your business and your brand for many years.

AFFILIATE COMMISSIONS

Tim Ferriss didn't bank on his book *The Four Hour Workweek* becoming a best-seller. He designed the book to generate revenue through affiliate links to the products and services mentioned in his book. If you don't have something to sell yourself, this is a relevant business model to consider. It's a variation on the "free book plus upsell." The expected revenue stream is not from the book itself, but from the upsell.

In *The Four Hour Workweek,* Tim Ferriss recommended various companies that facilitate hiring based in India or the Philippines, where the wages are lower than in North America. I don't know the details of his affiliate commission arrangements, but it is typical to receive between 10% and 50% commission. If a reader engaged a virtual assistant, that relationship could potentially span several months or years.

Amazon makes it easy to receive affiliate commissions. Reid Tracy, CEO of Hay House, shared that while people may go to Amazon to buy an e-book for $1.99, they get commissions on anything else purchased at that time—whether it's another book or a washing machine. So affiliate commissions can add up over time.

5. Speaking

SPEAKING IS ONE of the highest-paid professions in the world. Speakers speak for free—or for a fee. Fees range widely, and speakers can be handsomely rewarded whether they are speaking for a fee, or speaking for free and then selling their resources at the back of the room.

For example:

- $20,000 speaking fee × 50 engagements = $1,000,000
- $40,000 back-of-room sales × 25 gigs = $1,000,000
- $1,000 p.p. × 200 people × 5 retreats = $1,000,000

It is common for speakers with popular TED talks to command $20,000 USD or more per talk. Speaking fees vary widely, depending on the popularity of the topic and the celebrity status of the speaker. Famous authors such as Hilary Clinton can earn $200,000 per speaking engagement. Not bad for an hour of talking!

My friend Alex Carroll has sold over $1.4M of his self-published books by being a guest on radio shows. He now teaches others how to be a guest expert on radio and podcasts. When he speaks "for free" he often generates $40,000 by selling his resources at the back of the room. So speaking "for free" can be lucrative.

Virtually all popular public speakers are authors. The prosperous ones have a back-end business model. For example, Seth Godin's books promote his alt-MBA program, currently $3,850.

Dan Kennedy, speaker, copywriter, and author of the *No B.S.* series of books, has used his writings as lead magnets for years. His books launched his platform as a public speaker, where he has spoken alongside Zig Ziglar and Bill Clinton. Kennedy typically generated over a million dollars per year speaking-to-sell from the stage. His books attract clients to his copy-writing business, where he can potentially make over a million dollars in royalties per client.

Jack Canfield and Mark Victor Hansen were public speakers long before they were authors. Audiences loved the heart-warming stories, so Canfield and Hansen were convinced that people would enjoy reading the uplifting stories in a book. But publishers did not agree.

"*Chicken Soup for the Soul* was rejected by 144 publishers. If we had given up after 100 publishers, I likely would not be where I am now," said Jack Canfield, co-creator of the *Chicken Soup for the Soul* series of books.

Chicken Soup for the Soul became the best-selling trade paperback series of all time in 2008. Today, according to their web site: "*Chicken Soup for the Soul* receives hundreds of millions of monthly media impressions as a result of 5 weekly columns syndicated to newspapers by King Features, a radio network of over 200 radio stations covering over 65% of the United States, a blog network with over 9.5 million monthly unique visitors and press coverage."

Simply as authors, or only as speakers, they would not have been able to create a media franchise. But by combining media, they launched their business to the stratosphere and became wealthy. Jack Canfield went from being a high school teacher making $8,000 a year to making 10× that and then becoming a multimillionaire. Jack Canfield and Mark Victor Hansen did not merely write a book. They created a valuable brand.

If their first book had never been published, Jack Canfield and Mark Victor Hansen would have lost out on a fortune. They did not self-publish, so they lost out on a small fortune to their publisher (HCI) but gained the *Chicken Soup* brand.

In 2008, Jack Canfield and Mark Victor Hansen sold their company to a new ownership group. In 2017 this company, backed by movie star Aston Kutcher, launched an IPO (initial public offering) on the NASDAQ stock market with plans to raise $30 million, according to Inc. magazine. They have positioned the company as the "Netflix for inspirational content."

6. Training & Certification

PEOPLE WHO LIKE your book frequently want more. Online training and/or online membership sites enrich the material in your book and provide ongoing engagement and transformation.

Books often become the backbone for a certification program as others want to learn and become an accredited provider of the methods taught by the author.

For example:

- $10,000 training × 100 students = $1,000,000
- $2,000 training × 500 students = $1,000,000
- $500 annual membership × 2,000 = $1,000,000

Marie Kondo's KonMari Consultant training program costs about $2,000, plus $500 membership fee every year. Five hundred students would generate a million dollars a year. Ongoing memberships of two thousand students would produce a million dollars a year.

When I took my MBA in 2015, one of the books I read was *The New Rational Manager* by Charles Kepner and Benjamin Tregoe. Kepner-Tregoe offers various levels of certification, some at around $20,000. While this might seem a lot to invest in training, let's consider the ROI (return on investment).

Robert Lutz, former Vice Chairman at General Motors, said of the cash value of using the KT process, "It has to be in the tens, if not hundreds of millions of dollars. In terms of advancing my career and getting promoted, the value is probably worth several million dollars to me personally."

If, as Lutz indicated, the KT process saved hundreds of millions of dollars, then investing $20,000 for the KT training provides a phenomenal rate of return. Incidentally, Lutz has written several books, including *Icons and Idiots: Straight Talk on Leadership.*

My book, *From Heartbreak to Happiness*, launched the coach certification training program at the Grief Coach Academy.

Students benefit by learning my proven methods to coach their clients *From Heartbreak to Happiness®*. Typically, participants get the unexpected benefit that they release their own stress, heartbreak, trauma, or grief, and reclaim happiness, vitality, and joy.

I may do things accidentally the first time, but I do my best to catch the message. After discovering the full value of a book to launch a new program, I wrote *Marketing Fastrack.* People kept asking for my help with their marketing, and the book *Marketing Fastrack* empowered me to pivot from only helping coaches and grieving people to helping all kinds of entrepreneurs.

This book is designed to help experts, leaders, speakers, and entrepreneurs, obviously. I'm congruent with my message. I walk my talk.

In your book, you may choose to have fewer marketing messages—or more marketing messages. That's up to you, your business, and your goals.

7. Evergreen Bestseller

I'VE SAVED THE best for last. This is my favorite strategy.

For example:

- $100,000 per month × 12 months = $1,200,000

Having your eye on the long-term success of your book is the best strategy, but not for the apparent reason (book sales). I like this strategy because, provided you have implemented one or several of the business-building strategies outlined above, your business will be thriving as you promote your book.

With this revenue, you can afford to continue promoting your book until it hits the tipping point. Once your book has achieved the tipping point, other opportunities to launch a movement, influence the masses, and generate income open up, such as TV and movie deals.

To show you how it works, I will use Hal Elrod as an example. Elrod turned his self-published book *The Miracle Morning* into an evergreen bestseller. Let's look at his book as an example of what is possible with the consistent, ongoing promotion of a self-published book.

Elrod kept his eye on the prize of launching a movement. Unlike the majority focused on the sprint need to create massive sales in one week, Elrod devoted himself to the marathon of launching an evergreen bestseller. He did not want to be a blip with a one-time success and then be forgotten.

When his book was published, Elrod didn't have a platform. His book sold 2,000 copies when it was released, and then sales trickled off. Many authors would have given up. Not Elrod.

"When you believe in your message, you keep promoting and sharing it," said Elrod.

Elrod got media training so that he could be a guest expert on TV, radio, and podcasts. After a year and a half of steady promotion, the book hit a tipping point. After two years and over 200 podcast interviews, his book is steadily selling 10,000 copies per month (as of 2019). At a $6 profit per book, that's $60,000 profit every single month. That is an excellent ongoing revenue stream.

The Miracle Morning has launched a thriving business and a flourishing movement. Elrod designed *The Miracle Morning* to build a movement right from the start. While many authors neglect to provide a way for readers to engage with concepts in their book, Elrod made this a priority.

He created *The Miracle Morning* Facebook community, which now has over 40,000 members. Most books that have an opt-in achieve an 8% to 12% opt-in rate, but Elrod said he has a phenomenal 80% of readers choosing to opt-in and engage with his community. Over 500,000 people practice his method daily in more than countries. He has succeeded in launching a movement.

Elrod uses a hybrid publishing model, using publishers in foreign markets, and self-publishing in America. This allows him to have the best of both worlds, maximizing profit, and yet not sacrificing reach internationally. His book has been translated into 27 languages.

Most authors sabotage their success by not baking the marketing strategy into the book. That's like baking bread and forgetting to add the yeast. Once it is baked (published), it is too late. Think it through now.

The Miracle Morning has generated $1.2 million in royalties, according to Elrod. That doesn't include income from speaking, events, coaching, or sales of other products and services, so I expect this book has triggered 8 figures overall.

"Most great books change the way you think, but once you stop reading it, you stop thinking about it. But if it changes your behavior, it will change your life, and you will share it—if reminded to do so," said Elrod.

Many of last year's best-selling books are not on the best-selling charts this year. Don't focus on being a "blip" with short-term success. Build long-term success by writing a book that elicits behavior change, compels readers to opt-in and share, and creates a self-sustaining community. Then keep promoting your book—and your movement—forever.

The classic *The 7 Habits of Highly Effective People* by Stephen Covey was published in 1989 and has sold over 25 million copies. Although Covey died in 2012, book sales continue to generate over $200,000 per month.

The One Thing author Gary Keller is another example of providing bonuses to entice readers to engage and opt-in. His website offers free resources, including one-page PDFs, to help readers implement the concepts in his book. Done right, your email list will be worth far more than the initial book sale.

Tim Ferriss, author of *Tools of Titans*, said that he's grateful that one of his friends emphasized the importance of building an email list. Every podcast, Ferriss invites listeners to join his email list so they can receive "a little morsel of goodness" every Friday.

Social media platforms may change the rules, wipe out your followers, or delete your account, but you own your email list. You don't want to build your business on "rented land." Your email list is a valuable asset. Today, Ferriss can send an email blast to his list of fans and immediately trigger sales to fill an event or sell his latest book.

Body for Life author Bill Phillips created enormous engagement with his 12-week contest. People eagerly entered his 90-day challenge, vying for the prize of a red Ferrari. Their physical transformations were captured in compelling "before" and "after" pictures and featured on the attention-grabbing front cover of Body for Life. The result? Over $100 million in book sales, and $1.5 billion from Phillips-inspired brands over the past decade, according to Bill Phillips.

To launch an evergreen best-seller, engaging with your community is essential. Choose one thing and commit to doing it consistently. It could be a weekly email, a daily blog post, an every-other-day Facebook post, a weekly YouTube video, a bi-monthly podcast, or something else. Engaging consistently with your community creates connections and triggers trust.

10 KEYS TO CREATING AN EVERGREEN BEST-SELLER

1. Write a great book that sparks transformation.
2. Commit to being a great messenger for your message.
3. Get media training.
4. Step into the media spotlight.
5. Trigger new habits in your book.
6. Offer bonus resources to entice readers to opt-in and reinforce new habits.
7. Make it easy for readers to spread the word.
8. Provide a challenge to increase engagement.
9. Build an ongoing, engaged community.
10. Commit to ongoing promotion until your message has reached the masses.

In summary, with the right ongoing promotion and right call-to-action (CTA) in the right book, your book can become an evergreen bestseller, bringing you more and more revenue, clients, and media coverage over time. Your book builds your business and your brand.

Next, let's look at how successful authors write books more rapidly and effortlessly.

"Remember that every single thing that happened to you is yours, and you get to tell it. If people wanted you to write more warmly about them, they should've behaved better."

~ ANNE LAMOTT ~

7

YOUR LAUNCH

"Your ships come in only after you have sent them out."
~ Catherine Ponder ~

TO LAUNCH AS a Thought Leader and published author, you obviously need a book. Today, self-publishing is easier than ever. But writing is as hard as ever. That's a problem. What's the solution?

Tim Ferriss based his New York Times best-selling books *Tools of Titans* and *Tribe of Mentors* on his podcast interviews with movers and shakers.

Well-known authors turn talks into books. Before writing, Wayne Dyer and Ralph Waldo Emerson would repeatedly lecture on a topic to refine their thoughts and magnify audience reactions.

With over 100 million copies sold, and still ranked as one of the top business books 70 years after it was published, *Think and Grow Rich* resulted from Napoleon Hill interviewing leaders including Henry Ford, Charles M. Schwab, Thomas Edison, and Andrew Carnegie.

The classic best-seller *How to Win Friends and Influence People* was based on recordings of Dale Carnegie's lectures. (Apparently, Carnegie didn't think he had a book in him!)

DON'T WRITE. TALK

Thought Leader Arianna Huffington candidly revealed that her secret to writing 15 books in just a few years was to capture her thoughts on audio, and then delegate the rest.

Throughout history, the words of extraordinary people were captured and written down by someone else. Jesus, Buddha, and Socrates did not write books. Paul spread the words of Jesus. Plato shared Socrates's teaching. Monks passed down Buddha's philosophy. If not for scribes, their lessons would have been lost, impoverishing the world.

Thinking and writing are distinct skills. It is a different skill to write a poem, a screenplay, a newspaper article, a novel, a memoir, or a stirring speech.

Thinking is a multiplier. Sharing ideas multiplies their value. Leaders have thoughts, insights, expertise, and experiences worth sharing. That doesn't mean that they've spent 10,000 hours writing! Leaders are busy leading—not writing. Editors and writers are word-wranglers.

Jack Canfield's recent book, *The Success Principles*, was written by Janet Switzer; Blake Masters served as Peter Thiel's coauthor and scribe on *Zero to One*; Peter Diamandis teamed up with Steven Kotler to write *Abundance* and *Bold*.

Bill Moyers interviewed Joseph Campbell on a PBS special, which was turned into a must-read book for people in the film business, *The Power of Myth*. (George Lucas credits Joseph

Campbell's work to the structure and lasting success of the *Star Wars* movies.)

Suzanne Somers has a point of view about bio-identical hormones and wanted more gravitas than the former *Three's Company* star could command by herself. So she added interviews with leading experts to her books, including *Ageless: The Naked Truth About Bioidentical Hormones* and *Knockout: Interviews With Doctors Who Are Curing Cancer—And How To Prevent Getting It In The First Place*.

Autobiographies are typically based on a leader or celebrity talking to a writer. For example, Goldie Hawn's autobiography *A Lotus Grows in the Mud* is the result of Hawn talking to writer Wendy Holden. You'll often see the name of the Thought Leader first, then "as told to" before the name of the scribe.

Before announcing that they're running for President, it's common to see smart, ambitious politicians write a book (with a ghostwriter) and go on a book tour. A new book provides ready access to the media and the opportunity to be in the spotlight.

Million-Dollar Memoirs

GREAT BOOKS START and end with audio. Talking is the new writing. Listening is the new reading. Audiobooks are becoming more and more popular.

Hilary Clinton won a Grammy Award for the Best Spoken Word Album in 1997 for the audio recording of her 1996 book. *It Takes a Village*, and was nominated for a Grammy for her book *Living History*.

Clinton received an $8 million advance from the publisher for *Living History* and has made more than that from her paid public speeches. Apparently, she paid her ghostwriter $500,000.

"This book may not have taken a village to write, but it certainly took a superb team ... The smartest decision I made was to ask Lissa Muscatine, Maryanne Vollers and Ruby Shamir to spend two years of their lives working with me," wrote Clinton in the Acknowledgements section of *Living History*, giving a tip of her hat to Maryanne Vollers (ghostwriter), Lissa Muscatine (speechwriter) and Ruby Shamir (researcher).

Hilary Clinton is credited as the sole author of *Living History*. In contrast, Senator John Edwards and Senator John McCain both elected to credit their scribes on the cover of their books. Hilary Clinton received $14 million for her book *Hard Choices* released in 2014.

$60M FOR OBAMA MEMOIRS

Eclipsing Clinton's advance, Penguin Random House paid $60M for memoirs by Barack and Michelle Obama. Barack Obama's first memoir, *Dreams from My Father*, has already earned him over $15 million. In 2019, Michelle Obama was on tour for her book *Becoming* released in November 2018. Typically, revenue from book sales is a fraction of income from speaking engagements.

THE NOBEL PRIZE FOR LITERATURE

The 1953 Nobel Prize for Literature was awarded to Winston Churchill, which likely acknowledged both his writing and his stirring wartime speeches, which changed the course of history.

In *Mr. Churchill's Profession* Peter Clarke, formerly a history professor at Cambridge University, wrote that Churchill's first love was writing, and his writing career helped him become a powerful orator.

Churchill dictated his books aloud to his secretaries. "Dictation is the reason there was no economy in his writing. It's the old phrase that he 'didn't have time to make his books shorter.'" wrote Clarke.

Churchill's writing was so popular there was no way he could keep up with the demand without employing a team of writers, editors, secretaries, and researchers.

For example, in 1934, Churchill was commissioned to write by three newspapers and a magazine (*Daily Mail*, *News of the World*, *Sunday Dispatch*, and *Collier's*). The editor of the *Sunday Dispatch* hired journalist Adam Marshall Diston to rework Churchill's old material. At the same time, Churchill himself would write one new piece in every four published by the *Sunday Dispatch*.

Later, Churchill employed Diston directly as his ghostwriter. Churchill's private secretary, Edward Marsh, also worked as one of Churchill's ghostwriters.

Churchill could easily afford to pay for the help as he earned $100,000 a year (about $1.4 million in 2016 dollars) from his writing and lecturing. Churchill needed the money from writing to cover his considerable expenses keeping up Chartwell, his stately but rundown home.

Best-Selling Books

A SURPRISING NUMBER of excellent books started as interviews, and many well-known authors were initially self-published.

Many blockbuster books are built upon the foundation of conversations, interviews, or transcribed recordings. Some started as radio or podcast interviews (Ernest Holmes and Tim Ferriss), others began as audio recordings of lectures (Dale Carnegie), or a TV special (Joseph Campbell and Bill Moyers).

BEST-SELLING "SPOKEN AUTHOR" BOOKS

- *The Power of Myth* by Joseph Campbell and Bill Moyers
- *Think and Grow Rich* by Napoleon Hill
- *How to Win Friends and Influence People* by Dale Carnegie
- *Knockout* & *Ageless* by Suzanne Somers
- *A Lotus Grows in the Mud* by Goldie Hawn and Wendy Holden
- *The Power of This Thing Called Life* by Ernest Holmes
- *Thrive, On Becoming Fearless* by Arianna Huffington
- *Tools of Titans* and *Tribe of Mentors* by Tim Ferriss

Clear writing starts with speaking, not writing. Speaking aloud clarifies what works and what doesn't. That's one of the reasons my clients record videos and speak in front of a live audience. They get immediate feedback and improve rapidly. As a result, their thoughts become crystallized, and they become confident speakers ready for the spotlight.

The best books start and end with words spoken aloud. I read every page of a manuscript out loud to make sure that it sounds right. This catches over-written, circuitous, and unclear sentences. Seth Godin says that he writes like he talks, so he never suffers from writer's block. Like Hemingway, I believe that the best writing is invisible. I want the reader to notice the ideas, not the words.

BEST-SELLING SELF-PUBLISHED BOOKS

- *Your Erroneous Zones* (35 million copies)
- *Eragon* (30 million copies)
- *Rich Dad, Poor Dad* (26 million copies)
- *Can't Hurt Me* (20 million copies)
- *The Joy of Cooking* (18 million copies)
- *The Wealthy Barber*
- *The Celestine Prophesy*
- *Power vs. Force*
- *What Color is Your Parachute?*
- *The Tale of Peter Rabbit*
- *50 Shades of Grey*

BEST-SELLING SELF-PUBLISHED AUTHORS

- Benjamin Franklin
- Ralph Waldo Emerson
- Emily Dickinson
- Zane Grey
- Beatrix Potter
- Deepak Chopra
- Robert Kiyosaki
- e.e. cummings
- Marcel Proust
- Beatrix Potter
- James Redfield
- David Goggins
- Wayne Dyer

If you're an entrepreneur, giving your book to a large New York publisher makes no sense. It's like giving someone else control of your voice. You don't want to sacrifice your story or your marketing to the agenda of another business with vastly different interests.

Your book is a powerful lead magnet. It is the foundation of your author-ity, which brings us to your platform. Your platform is the engine that transforms your authority into results, including influence and income.

Tragically, most first-time authors don't think about their platform, and so they sabotage their long-term success. Getting published is not the end of the adventure. It is the beginning of an exciting new chapter. A book is a key. As everyone knows, to get the full value from a key, it needs to be used to open doors.

Your Platform

A BOOK IS not merely a book. A book is the price you pay to gain access to media coverage. It's like a Master's degree or PhD. Many people *could* get an MBA or a PhD—but few put in the effort. Your book is like that. Many people *could* write a book—but few take the time to distill their thoughts into a book. The fact that you have a degree—or a book—speaks volumes about you, and opens access to a higher playing field. Your book invites podcast hosts and TV producers into your world, as well as readers.

Thought Leaders are authors. But not every author is a Thought Leader. The difference? A platform. Building a viable platform requires more than a book. It deserves an overall marketing, messaging, and media plan.

Your book is like a match. You can use that match to start a fire if you apply it to the right fuel. But if you expect a match to light a bonfire all by itself, you're not setting yourself up for success.

What is a platform? The Merriam-Webster dictionary defines it as "a declaration of the principles on which a group of persons stands" and "a place or opportunity for public discussion."

Your book is a declaration of your principles and ideas. Next, create the opportunity for public discussion. Discussion reinforces your brand, builds your business, and builds your tribe of followers and fans.

5 YEARS OF STRUGGLE VS. 1 WEEKEND

Dr. Jennifer Herrera ("Dr. J") wanted to launch her platform, share her principles and ideas, and trigger a global discussion about a topic she was passionate about—education. She knew she needed a book, but found it almost impossible to carve out time to write. It wasn't her fault—she had her hands full running the four charter schools that she founded, Tucson International Academies, based in Arizona.

For the past ten years, 100% of her students have been accepted into college. Dr. J was instrumental in giving a better future to these young people. But she was heartbroken that other young people ended up in dead-end jobs because neither they—nor their parents—knew what was possible. She wanted to get her message out to the masses, so for five years, she had been struggling to write a book—but it was not even close to being completed.

Dr. J decided to stop struggling and get the support her message deserved. She enrolled in our Thought Leader Book Launch program, and I interviewed her as part of our book creation process in March of 2018. Here's what she shared on camera.

"There's nothing more frustrating than having a burning message that you want to share with people—to invite them into the mission and vision that you have—and not being able to complete it," said Dr. J. "Over the past two days with Aurora Winter, we've been able to complete the creative process on the book that I've been trying to write for **five years**. I'm so excited to see it come to fruition. I now have a completed project that I can share with others, my vision of *Making College Come True*."

Next, she took our media training, and her message became more polished. "The myth is that having a college degree is expensive. The truth is that **not** having a college degree is expensive," said Dr. J. "Over a lifetime, a college graduate typically earns a million dollars more than a high school graduate. Education is the key that opens many doors."

What was the result of Dr. J becoming a media-trained published author? Here's what Dr. J enthusiastically posted on Facebook:

"It's been just 7 weeks since my intensive mastermind with Aurora Winter in France where I made 4 videos, and my TV appearances have skyrocketed! I have been interviewed on 3 primary stations over 15 times in these 7 weeks, and they keep inviting me back! I am getting recognized in public now, and people have even stood in line to say hello to me. NEVER would I have predicted this attention! I even was noticed by the Mexican Consulate, and they have requested a special meeting with me. Thank you, Aurora. I encourage all of you to embrace Aurora's training. It works!!!"

Dr. J is using her new book *Making College Come True* to attract students to her charter schools, and attract clients for her coaching, speaking, and training services. She enjoyed the process of book creation so much that she is planning her second book already—*Making Business Come True*.

4 Phases to Launch

HERE IS AN overview of the four phases to launch a Thought Leader. A little later, I'll share the 10-step blueprint for creating, publishing, and promoting a Thought Leader's book.

Experts and entrepreneurs do the math. It yields a higher rate of return to focus on your core areas of expertise, and delegate the rest to expert interviewers, writers, editors, and designers. As a result, many busy leaders take advantage of our VIP done-for-you (DFY) Thought Leader Book Launch, including Greg Hammer, MD.

Dr. Greg Hammer is a professor of anesthesia and pediatrics at Stanford University, the chief of pediatric anesthesia research at Stanford University, and the CEO of MarteauMed. Greg's son, Max, was full of personality and full of life as a child. Max was joyful and present. Yet when he grew up, Max became troubled and distracted. He ruminated about the past and was anxious about the future. Max descended into a dark place.

Greg visited his son and urged him to come back home. As he and Max were texting back and forth about the best flights home, Max stopped responding. In a parent's worst nightmare, the police arrived at Greg's door and informed him that his beloved son was dead.

Deep in his own grief, Greg thought about how elusive happiness seems to be. So many people are happy as children, yet turn into anxious, self-conscious adults. What could he do to turn this tide of human misery?

An antidote to suffering and a practical, step-by-step path to well-being emerged, first as a meditation practice, and later as the idea for a book, *GAIN Without Pain*, with G being for gratitude, A being for Acceptance, I being for Intention, and N being for Nonjudgement.

Greg's book idea stayed dormant—tugging at his heart—until we met. He decided to get support and joined our Thought Leader Book Launch program. By delegating parts of the process, he was freed to express his words, experience, and ideas. Same Page LLC (my company) published his book *GAIN Without Pain* on May 15, 2020.

We did the book launch for his book. The result that it quickly became a #1 New Release on Amazon (Medicine & Psychology) and became a #1 Bestseller in just four days. For a first-time, unknown author without an email list or a social media following, this was a great success. *GAIN Without Pain* also won an IPPY award for excellence. I presented Greg with a bottle of champagne to celebrate this good news. Now he has bragging rights forever. These accolades will help him with his next book and his fees as a speaker.

Next, I will outline the four phases of launching a book and Thought Leader. This is what we do for our Thought Leader Book Launch clients. You could follow this outline and do these tasks yourself, or apply to join our exclusive Thought Leader programs and get our support.

Overview

The right book is the key that opens many doors. A book establishes your leadership and authority. Most first-time authors make rookie mistakes and unwittingly sabotage their success. Your book is the highest-leverage asset to launch your platform.

We have a proven book creation, publication, and launch service for leaders and entrepreneurs who have a message they want to share with the world. Here is an overview of the four phases.

I. Book Creation

Most leaders are too busy to carve out the time to write a book. Instead of spending years (typically 3—5 years!) struggling to write, edit, and launch your book, you spend a weekend. It's a half-day of preparation, followed by a day being interviewed for your book. Live training and online video training walk you through each step of the process. We hold your hand every step of the way with one-on-one phone calls and emails to round out the process. This process creates a manuscript in your own words that flows in an engaging conversational style.
Outcome: Your Manuscript

II. Evergreen Bestseller Program

We don't just want to create a book—we want to create a platform to launch your success to the next level. In this next phase, we layer in your specific goals and objectives. We add in elements essential to an evergreen bestseller. A professional, eye-catching book is designed with an eye-catching cover and elegant interior layout. Phone calls and emails round out the process to reflect your preferences. We create a book launch plan tailored to achieve your goals.
Outcome: Your Book in Your Hands

III. Media Magnet

Your book is an opportunity for media coverage that could reach millions of people. Media training prepares you to be interviewed as a guest expert on radio, TV, podcasts. It polishes your message so you can speak on stages such as TEDx. During a VIP day, we shoot videos to create a video marketing funnel to promote your new book and platform. Phone calls and emails round out the process.

Outcome: Media-Ready, Videos Created

IV. Launch

Now we deploy the assets created to launch you as a Thought Leader. Several press releases are broadcast, with guaranteed pickup by 100 media outlets. We create an online press kit that showcases you, your book, your content, your videos, and your mission. With your input, we create a turn-key media interview for producers. Time to plan your book launch party!

Outcome: Thought Leader Launched!

10-Step Launch Blueprint

NEXT, I'LL PULL back the curtain and give you our 10-step blueprint for success. These are the 10 steps required to create, publish, and launch a book and Thought Leader. You could follow this step-by-step process and do this yourself.

Most successful leaders would rather delegate, or at least have a mentor to help guide them step-by-step. You can apply to join one of our exclusive Thought Leader programs and get our help to achieve your goals more rapidly and efficiently.

1. STRATEGIC PLAN: BEGIN WITH THE END IN MIND

This critical first step is missing from the traditional publishing model. We consult with you and identify the ideal strategy for your business, your brand, and your book. We discover creative gold in your personal and professional story.

We discern the kind of book that will increase your income and influence. We identify your ideal path to becoming recognized and respected as a Thought Leader in your industry. If you have a draft manuscript, we take a look at that. After a half-dozen calls with you (typically via video conference on Zoom), we agree on an overall vision for your book.

2. TRAINING: WE HELP YOU CREATE A CLEAR, COMPELLING MESSAGE

We've discovered that the fastest way for you to clarify your message is to shoot short videos following our story structure recipes. This secret shortcut enhances your confidence as a public speaker while simultaneously building a better book. (As a bonus, the videos can become the backbone of your video marketing funnel.)

Our unique *Thought Leader Launch*™ process means that anyone who can talk can create an excellent book. Most first-time authors just start writing—which is like throwing together a mundane dinner from whatever happens to be in the fridge. Our process is like training with a chef from Le Cordon Bleu, creating a master meal plan, then going shopping at the farmer's market for the finest, freshest, organic ingredients to create something delightful.

Mentoring, training, and masterminding provide a rich, stimulating, and supportive environment. You can join the instruction from the convenience of your own home, as the training is provided by live videoconference on Zoom. Ample online videos allow you to learn 24-7, and our online community offers support and masterminding. Coaching and masterminding is also provided at live in-person events. Every week you get help developing your ideas, stories, and business strategy.

3. OUTLINE: YOUR TITLE, KEY POINTS, SIGNATURE STORY & MORE

Next, a framework for the structure of your book is outlined. The outline includes your big idea, your key points, your signature story, your myth busts, your brand story, your creation story, your client success stories, and more. Fortunately, the training modules reveal the successful structure of each of these essential elements. By now, your manuscript has a working title and subtitle.

4. INTERVIEW: YOUR EXPERTISE & EXPERIENCE, PASSION & PURPOSE

Your book contains your ideas, expertise, and experience. You share your thoughts and stories in response to interview questions. Every author we have worked with so far has discovered that the interview process is surprisingly easy and fun.

Typically, the interview is done in person over a day or two, however it can also be done on Zoom or over the phone. Select VIP clients benefit from being interviewed by me (Aurora Winter) personally; otherwise an experienced editor who resonates with your topic is provided. The interview captures your words, your ideas, and your stories. If you prefer, you can submit your draft manuscript, and we can start from there. You are the author.

5. EDITING: PROFESSIONAL EDITING

The audios from your interview are transcribed, but they still need a lot of work to become a polished manuscript. If you have provided a draft manuscript, it goes through the same editing process. Fortunately, this painstaking line-by-line word-by-word editing is not your responsibility.

Professional editing is next. Published authors, as well as editors who have worked for respected publications (such as *The New York Times*, *The Wall Street Journal*, or *WIRED* magazine), are on our team to ensure that your words become a polished manuscript.

6. EVERGREEN BESTSELLER PROGRAM

While other small publishers may hype creating a New York Times best-seller, the truth is that a blip of sales for one week is **not** the key to lasting success. The key to lasting success is an evergreen bestseller that builds your business and your brand for many years. The goal is to position you as a Thought Leader, not merely publish a book. In this phase, we layer in elements to make your message "stickier" and more profitable. We create a book launch plan tailored to achieve your goals.

7. COVER & INTERIOR DESIGN, FIVE STAR BRAND REVIEW

Your book is a vital part of your brand. A book is judged by its cover, so we want a stellar cover for your book. We review and refine the working title and subtitle at this point. Compelling copy is written for the back cover. Professional designers create several eye-catching book covers so that you can select your preferred option. You retain copyright, ownership, and control.

8. MEDIA TRAINING: LIGHTS, CAMERA, ACTION!

We set you up for success as a speaker, presenter, and guest expert. Media training prepares you to speak on stages (such as TED) or be interviewed on podcasts and broadcasts. Your book creates the opportunity for media coverage that could reach millions of people and create a tipping point for you, your business, and your brand.

Typically, we shoot videos to promote you, your business, and your new book at our annual Podium Power event. Several of our clients have practiced their TED talk at one of our events, and then delivered their actual presentation on a TEDx stage a few days or weeks later. Why not you? This is your time to shine.

9. LAUNCH

You are now ready to be interviewed and leverage podcasts and broadcasts to get your message out to the masses. In this phase, we deploy the assets created to launch you as a Thought Leader. These assets include an online press kit that showcases you, your book, your content, your videos, and your mission. Your book is turned into a hook—a show pitch.

Media hosts and producers alike will book a media-trained author who delivers engaging content that provides immediate value to their audience—not an advertisement for a book. As a guest expert, you can benefit from media coverage without having to pay for advertising.

For example, one of the reasons that Greg Hammer's book was the #1 New Release on Amazon was that he took our media training and was featured on TV and radio interviews that our team scheduled on his behalf.

10. ONGOING SUPPORT

We provide training, mentoring, masterminding, and live events throughout the process to support you and create the best outcome. After your book has been published, we typically interview you so that your message reaches even more people. We hold your hand every step of the way as you step into the spotlight as an author and Thought Leader.

Promoting your book, your brand, and your business is an ongoing process like gardening. Your brand is like a beautiful orchard. Your business is the process of nurturing and harvesting that orchard. Your book is like a grove of apple trees. It can yield a more bountiful harvest year after year.

Typically, authors toil writing their books for years. If you'd like to focus on the things you do best and delegate the rest, apply for our done-for-you Thought Leader Book Launch program. Or join our Million-Dollar Message training and get support doing it yourself. Schedule a complimentary business breakthrough call and learn more here: www.BookCall.biz.

"Success action is cumulative in its results."
~ Wallace Wattles ~

8 YOUR COACH

"Surround yourself with people who are going to lift you higher."
~ Oprah Winfrey ~

THE RAPID RATE of technological change means that you need to run as fast as you can just to stay in the same place, to paraphrase the Red Queen from *Alice in Wonderland*. Now more than ever before, we need to surround ourselves with people who lift us higher.

Angel investor and co-creator of the Facebook platform, Dave Morin, shared his concerns about the rising tide of people feeling depressed and anxious. On the podcast, *This Week in Startups,* Jason Calacanis asked him, "How can people reduce stress?"

"**Number one you should have a coach.** Number one, out of the gate. **If you're a Founder, you need to treat yourself like an Olympic athlete.** Whether you're a Warriors athlete or an Olympic athlete that's in a solo sport, you don't go into it without a coach," said Morin.

"If you actually talk to professional athletes, they've got mediation coaches and yoga coaches and a masseuse and a nutritionist, all kinds of things. I think Founders need to take it a lot more seriously... We give people an enormous amount of money to fill their company's bank account with millions of dollars. They've never managed that before. That's an instant pressure cooker."

A coach is like a safety valve on a pressure cooker, preventing explosions. By providing a calm sounding board, a good coach helps you avoid making disastrous decisions in the heat of the moment. Surrounding yourself with a supportive group of people increases health, happiness, longevity, productivity, and profit.

Google CEO "Everyone Needs A Coach"

"EVERYONE NEEDS A coach," said Eric Schmidt, who joined Google in 2001 and helped the company grow from a Silicon Valley startup to a global leader in technology. He served as Google's CEO from 2001—2011 and Executive Chairman from 2011-2018, alongside founders Sergey Brin and Larry Page.

DON'T BE "TONE DEAF"

"When you have a hyper-analytical person, which I am, and which many people in my industry are, you can be tone-deaf. And anything that you can do to increase your understanding, if you're like me, of how people are going to react to things, how people will perceive emotionally what you're doing is helpful. When we started at Google, we would just throw things out—we didn't worry about what impact they had. Maybe they worked, maybe they didn't. ... Businesses are more than products and facts. They are about people and emotion, and morality. You have to really think about it," shared Schmidt during his April 2019 interview on *The Tim Ferriss Show*.

Tim Ferriss asked, "If you were to give advice to someone looking for a business coach, how would you tell them how to vet candidates?"

"Coaching is a special skill—it's like writing. There are people who are great writers. There are people who are great coaches," said Eric Schmidt, co-author of *Trillion Dollar Coach: The Leadership Playbook of Silicon Valley's Bill Campbell.* "The first question is: Is this a person who lights up a room? Is this a person who has that natural charisma that people want to listen to? Is this a person we can get to be part of our team? Coaching is a highly, highly personal thing. When you have a great coach, you love your coach. Go back to athletics. People talk about their coaches in reverential terms because they get them to perform so well."

Tim Ferriss has a business coach. "Even if you have a small organization—even if you *are* your organization—**having a coach to hold you accountable and force you to clarify your thinking is so leveraged and valuable.**"

Talent Isn't Born. It's Grown.

HAVE YOU EVER wondered why history encompasses fertile periods rich with innovation, art, architecture, music, and creativity—such as the Renaissance—and other periods which were barren, such as the Dark Ages? What creates this flux? Do specific conditions trigger greatness? And if so, how can we deliberately create conditions that foster talent?

CLUSTERS OF GENIUS

David Banks, a Carnegie Mellon University statistician, wrote a paper entitled *The Problem of Excess Genius*. Curiously, geniuses are not scattered uniformly through history and geography. Instead, they appeared in clusters.

"The most important question we can ask of historians is, 'Why are some periods and places so astonishingly more productive than the rest?'" Banks wrote. "It is intellectually embarrassing that this is almost never posed squarely ... although its answer would have thrilling implications for education, politics, science, and art."

Banks identified several flourishing clusters: Florence (from 1440 to 1490), Athens (from 440 B.C. to 380 B.C.), and London (from 1570 to 1640).

Let's consider Florence, where I hosted my Thought Leader Mastermind retreat in 2019. In 1490, Florence had a population estimated at 70,000—equivalent to that of modern-day Palo Alto, California. In just a few generations, Florence produced a dazzling outpouring of innovation and artistic accomplishment.

Leonardo da Vinci provides a brilliant example. Famous for painting the *Mona Lisa* and *The Last Supper*, he also conceived engineering ideas ahead of his time, including the helicopter, parachute, tank, calculator, and the double hull. This Italian polymath advanced the fields of engineering, mathematics, chemistry, physics, hydrodynamics, botany, art, and architecture. Leonardo da Vinci's lifetime of prolific creation and innovation started at the age of twelve when da Vinci was sent to Florence to apprentice under Verrocchio.

Leonardo da Vinci was not the only genius. Florence generated dozens of geniuses within two generations, including Donatello,

Giotto, Verrocchio, Caravaggio, Raphael, and Michelangelo. What was going on? Mentoring.

Craft Guilds were the norm in Florence at that time and they were talent factories. Guilds were built on the apprenticeship system. Youth apprenticed directly under the master's guidance and supervision. Apprentices struggled for thousands of hours painting, drawing, sculpting under the watchful eye of a master.

The youth were not engaged in theory, talking about a topic. Instead, but were **actively engaged doing** those tasks. They were observing and emulating others who were more skilled and experienced. The apprentices received immediate feedback to correct their errors and refine their techniques.

To make this example more relatable to today's world, imagine an eleven-year – intern. This lucky intern works under a Hollywood producer, author, and actor. The intern reads scripts, talks to actors, checks lighting on body doubles, sees various versions of the same film in rough cut, observes how the director works with actors, and sees first-hand how editing and music transform raw footage into brilliant entertainment. Would it be a surprise that this intern would one day become a star? Not at all. Think of Goldie Hawn and her daughter Kate Hudson, actress, fashion designer, and author.

INSTALL BROADBAND IN YOUR BRAIN

You can upgrade the speed of your operating system from strolling along at a grandmotherly pace of two miles an hour to 200 miles an hour, the speed of a Formula One racing car! That's an astonishing 100-fold improvement.

Want to upgrade your internal operating system by 100×? Deep practice is the answer. As you focus with intensity on the outer edges of your comfort zone, you are rewiring your brain. You are paving neural super highways where there were only dirt trails before.

In his first-rate book, *The Talent Code: Greatness Isn't Born. It's Grown,* Daniel Coyle identified myelin as the holy grail of growing talent. Let's hear from Coyle to understand the science behind growing skill and myelin.

He wrote, "Every human skill, whether it's playing baseball or playing Bach, is created by chains of nerve fibers carrying a tiny electrical impulse—basically, a signal traveling through a circuit. Myelin's vital role is to wrap those nerve fibers the same way that rubber insulation wraps a copper wire, making the signal stronger and faster by preventing the electrical impulses from leaking out. When we fire our circuits in the right way—when we practice swinging that bat or playing that note—our myelin responds by wrapping layers of insulation around that neural circuit, each new layer adding a bit more skill and speed. The thicker the myelin gets, the better it insulates, and the faster and more accurate our movements and thoughts become."

Myelin is the foundation of all kinds of skills, both mental and physical. You can grow myelin at any age. Like a plant, myelin is alive. It doesn't shrink—but it can wither and die with neglect. Use it or lose it.

3 STEPS TO MASTERY

Three key factors grow talent:

1. Decide
2. Practice
3. Be Coached

For an exponential explosion of talent, you need all three elements.

1. Decide

The first step is a decision. It's ambition, a vision, a goal, a passion, a purpose. It's turning on the engine.

Potential without ignition is inert. Without desire, you're like a beautiful red Ferrari parked in your driveway. Without the key, it might as well be a statue. It's not going anywhere.

But with a big enough reason why people can achieve almost anything. As Thoreau said, "Go confidently in the direction of your dreams! Live the life you've imaged."

2. Practice

Intense practice leads to mastery. To expand your skills, you need to practice intently with focus and determination. Beware the comfort zone—there is no growth there. Instead, focus on the outside edge of your expertise. You want to practice under pressure.

Before you deliver your TED talk on stage, practice it in front of a live audience. That accelerates mastery.

To help my clients prepare for TV interviews, I role-play interviewing them at the front of the room at our events. When I teach a new communication recipe, it is not enough for my clients to intellectually grasp the material. Instead, they need to engage with the method and grow myelin by taking action. For example, shooting a video using that communication recipe, then submitting it for feedback for improvement. Shooting videos with their new content enhances confidence on-camera, improves the clarity of their message, and strengthens presentation skills.

TEDx speaker and author Diane Burton shared the difference that coaching has made in her life and business, "Aurora Winter has made a huge difference in my life. When she was coaching me, she helped me release something that had been holding me back for decades. With her encouragement, I wrote a book. In October of 2018, she coached me to do a TEDx talk—7 weeks later, I was standing on a stage presenting my TEDx! Aurora is now helping me leverage my popular TEDx talk to grow my business and make a bigger difference. I've already been featured in a magazine and on the media. Aurora is very strategic, innovative, and creative. She is an excellent business mentor and trainer. She's also an insightful, kind, and encouraging person. If you're looking for someone special to help you grow your income, influence, and impact, I highly recommend Aurora!"

3. Be Coached

The best way to grow talent is training under a coach or mentor. The coach needs to be someone who has demonstrated mastery in the area you're seeking to improve. Otherwise, you will be practicing your mistakes. If you want to improve your golf game or your tennis game, work with a pro. Often the hardest part is un-learning the mistakes you had practiced when you tried to learn it on your own.

For example, if you want to write and publish a book, work with a mentor who has expertise in writing and publishing books. If you want to grow your business, work with a mentor who has successfully grown several businesses. If you want to appear as a guest expert on TV, radio, and podcasts, then work with a mentor who has experience performing as a guest expert on media.

All talent hotbeds work on the same underlying principles. As Dr. George Bartzokis, a UCLA neurologist and myelin researcher, put it, "All skills, all language, all music, all movements, are made of living circuits, and all circuits grow according to certain rules."

The myth is that superstars achieve success alone. The fact is that superstars achieve success with support. Determined action under the guidance of a mentor builds mastery.

Watch the bonus video *Key to Automatic Success* to learn more about growing your talent and business: www.ThoughtLeaderBonuses.com

FROM RAGS TO RICHES

Jack Canfield

The co-creator of the *Chicken Soup for the Soul* series of books was once a struggling high school teacher making $8,000 a year. Now a multi-millionaire and in-demand keynote speaker, Canfield can generate $60,000 for a one-hour talk—7× more than he earned in an entire **year** as a teacher. He's still teaching, but his audience has changed, and his income and impact have skyrocketed.

His mentor: Self-made billionaire W. CLEMENT STONE, who was a businessman, philanthropist, and author.

Celine Dion

She was once an unknown, shy girl, surrounded by talented older sisters. Now a superstar, she is and one of the most famous Canadian singers of all time.

Her mentor: Music industry pro, RENÉ ANGÉLIL, who later became her husband. Rene developed her talent, introduced her to music-industry power brokers, and championed her career, with the result that her albums have sold millions of copies.

Tony Robbins

Robbins lived in a tiny studio apartment that was so small he had to do the dishes in the bathtub. One day, he came home to an eviction notice, he tore it off the door and flipped on the light to read it—but the power was shut off as he had not paid the electric bill. That rock bottom experience ignited a burning determination to find a better way.

Fast-forward to 2020. Robbins has reached 50 million people, has an empire generating billions, and hosts events packed with fans. A charismatic public speaker, he has a popular TED talk, a documentary feature film *I Am Not Your Guru,* and many books that inspire and inform his followers. Once the recipient of charity, Robbins has not forgotten his humble roots and now funds a charity that feeds the hungry. Robbins truly went from rock bottom to rock star. The tipping point was having a mentor.

His mentor: JIM ROHN, a Thought Leader and author who hosted transformative events (and showed young Robbins the ropes). A number of influential people acknowledge Jim Rohn's influence on their thinking and success, including Brian Tracy and T. Harv Eker. Rohn credits his mentor, John Earl Shoaf, with setting him on the path to success.

Jim Rohn said, "You are the average of the five people you spend the most time with." My mother echoed that warning, and yours likely did, too. Mother was right.

"Show me your friends, and I'll show you your future" is a modern concept with ancient roots. King Solomon warned, "He that walketh with wise men shall be wise: but a companion of fools shall be destroyed." (*Proverbs 13:20*).

WARNING: YOU BECOME LIKE YOUR FRIENDS

David Burkus, the author of *Friend of a Friend,* shared new research that underscores how deeply we are influenced by our friends, associates, and the friends of our friends. The Framingham Heart Study is one of the largest and longest-running health studies ever, containing a rich mine of data spanning three decades and thousands of people.

Nicholas Christakis and James Fowler mined that data to learn more about the breadth of social influence. The data revealed that if your friend becomes obese, you are 45% percent more likely to pack on the pounds yourself!

Shockingly, if a friend of your friend becomes obese, you are 20% more likely to gain weight —even if you don't know that friend of a friend. And if their friend becomes obese—that's someone three circles of friendship removed from you—then you are 10% more likely to gain weight than random chance. Your friends can make you fat—and so can their friends and their friends of friends.

This correlation is not limited to obesity but extends to other factors, such as smoking and happiness. For example, if your friend smokes, you are 61% more likely to be a smoker. If your friends are happy, you are likely to be happier. We rise or fall to what we see as normal.

How to Get a Million-Dollar Mindset...Fast!

KNOWING THE INFLUENCE of expectations, I joined a mastermind group of successful entrepreneurs after completing my MBA in 2015. I wanted to quickly shift my norm from a struggling-student mindset to a million-dollar mindset. I invested about $50,000 with a mentor to upgrade my thinking, skills, and friends. That was a nerve-wracking expenditure, especially on the heels of paying for my MBA and taking so much time off work to get it.

But soon, it felt normal to generate $50,000 to $100,000 a month. As a result, my income quickly increased to a "new normal," and I generated $250,000 of new business in 90 days. Investing in a mentor and joining a mastermind produced a much faster return on investment (ROI) than taking my MBA. Mindset trumps theory—especially when coupled with massive action.

The author of wildly successful *You Are a Badass* series of books, Jen Sincero, struggled for years, barely making ends meet, living the life of the starving artist in a converted garage. One day she hit the wall—she had had enough of poverty and coupon-clipping! She decided that she was going to do whatever it took to get rich.

She realized that she needed some new friends, as her current friends were all starving artists—just like her. (Are you starting to see a pattern?) Sincero said that she had to buy new friends—because she needed a new normal, one where thriving rather than struggling was routine. The scariest and most important decision she made was to borrow money and invest $85,000 to work with a mentor. That changed everything. She followed the mentor's advice, took action, and surrounded herself with other ambitious entrepreneurs. Her income immediately tripled (from $30,000 to $100,000 in a year). Now she's a popular speaker, has several *New York Times* best-selling books, and a thriving business.

Napoleon Hill studied the success habits of business tycoons and shared his findings in the classic best-seller *Think and Grow Rich*. Hill wrote that Henry Ford was handicapped by poverty, illiteracy, and ignorance when he began in business. Ford overcame these challenges and became one of the richest men in America. Ford's outstanding achievements were the result of befriending and masterminding with successful people such as Thomas A. Edison, Harvey Firestone, John Burroughs, and Luther Burbank.

Napoleon Hill wrote (caps are his): "Men take on the nature and the habits and the POWER OF THOUGHT of those with whom they associate in a spirit of sympathy and harmony. Leveraging the power of other minds, the "Master Mind" principle, was the foundation of business success... GREAT POWER CAN BE ACCUMULATED THROUGH NO OTHER PRINCIPLE!"

CHOOSING THE RIGHT COACH OR MENTOR

Robinson Smith, MBA, had a thriving 7-figure business as an investment advisor based in Victoria, BC, Canada. But after his father died, he found his passion waning. Something was missing.

He wanted to reach more people, make a bigger difference, and educate adults and youth about financial literacy. He decided to sell his business, write a book, and become an author and speaker.

Smith wrote, "When I decided to sell my successful business, I wanted to get a jump-start on starting something new. I decided to find a mentor who could help me launch my new business. Aurora Winter has accelerated my success immeasurably. I refined my business strategy, polished my presentation skills, wrote a book, and learned how to leverage media coverage. My new business is off to a great start as a result. Thanks to Aurora, it is much more than what I first thought it would be—what I ever thought it could be. If you are looking for a strategic coach, business mentor, or media trainer, I highly recommend Aurora."

If you're a Canadian homeowner, you would benefit from reading Smith's new book, *Master Your Mortgage for Financial Freedom*, which shows Canadian homeowners how to enjoy the same tax benefits American homeowners take for granted—tax-deductible mortgage interest.

Robinson Smith is currently refining his TED talk about the *Psychology of Money*, thanks to the experience of presenting it to a live audience at our Thought Leader Mastermind in Florence, Italy. The deadline, dress rehearsal, video replay, and live feedback all helped him improve his talk. He will be more polished and powerful when he steps onto the red carpet on the TED stage.

Another client, Dr. Tracy Thomas leveraged our Thought Leader Mastermind in Florence, Italy to rehearse her own TEDx talk, which she successfully presented a few weeks later. Diane Burton leveraged a Mastermind event I hosted in Half-Moon Bay, California to practice the TEDx talk she delivered 10 days after the retreat. Dhyanis Carniglia and Heidi Smith started writing their books at the Thought Leader Mastermind I hosted in San Miguel de Allende, Mexico, in February, 2020. Masterminds quicken dormant potential.

5 TIPS FOR FINDING YOUR MENTOR

1. Choose someone who sees greatness in you.
2. Choose someone aligned with your vision.
3. Choose a mentor who challenges you to grow.
4. Choose someone with a proven track record of success over several businesses and decades.
5. Choose a mentor you like, respect, and admire.

A common mistake is following the advice of multiple mentors simultaneously. That's like following half the recipe for chocolate cake and half the recipe for beef chili. Either recipe can produce excellent results—but half of each recipe does not work. Choose your coach wisely, then buckle down and do the work.

THE THOUGHT LEADER COACH

I love launching Thought Leaders. It gives me immense joy. It's the intersection of my areas of expertise and enthusiasm, which are:

- Entrepreneurship
- Storytelling
- Coaching

Entrepreneurship

I've been an entrepreneur my whole life and have launched three different business in three different industries, each of which generated 7 figures. Marketing is story selling.

Storytelling

I've been entranced by storytelling since I was nine. I have written six books and numerous screenplays. I spent a decade as a film and TV writer-producer, overseeing hundreds of hours of film and TV production and a development budget of over a million dollars. Now I help leaders create their own Million-Dollar Message.

Coaching

Igniting the greatness in others is part of my character. Nothing gives me more joy than being a catalyst for someone to create, communicate, and claim a life of joyful contribution. I have coaching and training coaches for over a decade.

I see entrepreneurs as the most promising answer to the world's most pressing problems. So, I'm choosing to devote my energy to launching Thought Leader entrepreneurs, using my extensive experience as an entrepreneur, storyteller, and coach.

Many people want to work with me as their coach. If that interests you, I work with people making a difference, including:

- Professionals with business insights to share
- Leaders who want to leave a legacy
- People who have a story to share
- Entrepreneurs pitching to raise capital
- People pivoting to their next chapter or next business
- Companies training their teams

Outstanding communication skills are needed to launch a movement, lead a winning team, leverage media coverage, or raise capital. We can help.

Typically, we combine coaching, training, and masterminding to deliver rapid results. Masterminding is a proven way to accelerate success. Many leaders struggle alone but thrive in a supportive group of like-minded leaders and ambitious entrepreneurs. To find out how we can help you launch as a Thought Leader, book a business breakthrough call at www.BookCall.biz. Get your complimentary *Thought Leader Launch* starter library with videos, audios, and more here: www.ThoughtLeaderLaunch.com.

"I remember saying to my mentor, "If I had more money, I would have a better plan. He responded quickly, "If you had a better plan, you'd have more money." You see, it's not the amount that counts; it's the plan that counts."

~ Jim Rohn ~

9

YOUR PURPOSE

"It turns out that a book is more durable than stone. It's more durable than a castle. It's more durable than an empire. And that's really interesting."
~ Jordan Peterson ~

THE FIRST TIME I met Dr. Wayne Dyer, I remember being enveloped in his warm and welcoming hug. He was my mentor and made a difference to me on many fronts, including endorsing my first book.

Today, Wayne Dyer is dead. Yet I still listen to his guiding voice on YouTube. I'm reading his book *I Can See Clearly Now* today, yet he died August 29, 2015.

My mother, Dorothy Lawton, died on January 13, 2016. Yet her guiding words still live on in my heart and mind. And not just in my mind, but in the audio recordings I made when I interviewed her several times in 2014. As time passes and memories fade, those interviews become more and more precious. She was born in 1933 and shared stories that I would like my yet-to-be-born grandchildren to hear. They will be incredulous that someone could grow up without the technology we take for granted today (no electricity, internet, car, computer or phone in her youth).

Her stories about love, learning, and life will allow my grandchildren to know their great-grandmother, and through her, to know their history and themselves more deeply. One of her favorite sayings was, "Beware the comfort zone—there's no growth there." Timeless advice.

IMMORTAL WORDS

The words of C. S. Lewis, Emily Dickenson, Ralph Waldo Emerson, Louisa May Alcott, Lao Tsu, Harper Lee, Shakespeare, Agatha Christie, J. R. R. Tolkien, Maya Angelou, Napoleon Hill, and many other authors continue to influence readers.

The brands of Mary Kay, Dale Carnegie, Julia Child, Werner Erhard, Louise Hay, Buckminster Fuller, Agatha Christie, Henry Ford, Coco Chanel, and others continue to thrive and support businesses today, in spite of the death of the visionary instigator.

Most people over-estimate what they can do in a year, but underestimate the difference that they can make in a lifetime.

The bible has lasted two thousand years. The words of Lao Tsu, Rumi, and Kahlil Gibran have influenced people for many generations.

Your book is part of your legacy. As Oprah Winfrey said, "Your legacy is every life you touch."

OVERCOMING LEGACY-KILLERS

People argue for their limitations. Other people can write books, do a TED talk, launch a startup, host a podcast, leave a legacy. But not me. My life history disqualifies me. My business track record invalidates me. I'm Clark Kent—not Superman. I don't have a degree. I'm too young. I'm too old.

People hide from their greatness with a shield of excuses: I'm too busy, I don't have the money, I don't have the time, I need to think about it, I'll do it later. "Later" turns into never.

The best way through this minefield of devastating doubt is to release the emergency brake and step on the gas. For goodness sake, get your foot off the brakes!

Brakes are caused by breaks, interestingly. By times when your worldview shattered. Trauma, betrayal, failures, disappointments, divorce, death, disease, and other setbacks trigger intense feelings—such as grief, shame, guilt, fear, and injured pride. People can conclude that they are deeply flawed. Of course you're flawed! Everyone's flawed. That's what makes you interesting!

Do the thing, and you will have the power. Shirk it, and you will be disempowered. We create our own Kryptonite.

"Turning on the gas" means connecting to your North Star, your big why, and unlocking your Superpowers.

"Release the brakes" means to master your emotions so that you can feel the fear and do it anyway. You can never entirely banish fear. Your ancient reptilian brain or "croc brain" evolved millions of years ago. Its job is to protect you from being mauled to death by a grizzly bear.

Unfortunately, your croc brain responds to threats to your pride as threats to your actual survival. Once triggered, it floods your body with hormones and activates the mighty "fight, flight or freeze" response. Hormones hijack your higher-level thinking and derail your plans.

You must practice to become formidable under pressure. Otherwise, the croc brain does will hijack your brain! You need to rewrite the default programming.

The croc brain has a fixed mindset. It does not understand your capacity to grow and learn. It does not care that mastery requires 10,000 hours—which means putting in 9,000 suboptimal hours. If left in charge, your reptilian brain will keep you stuck. Master your croc brain—or it will master you.

It is up to you to expand your capabilities, explore your interests, download creative ideas, make a difference, and boldly claim your destiny. Mastery is an ongoing process of learning and growing—it is not pre-installed. Learning inevitably involves missing the mark, course correcting, and trying again and again and again—until the new skill is gained. These common limiting beliefs sabotage success:

- Loss/Trauma—*My cracked foundation means I'm broken and unworthy.*
- Imposter Syndrome—*If people really knew me, they would reject me for my shortcomings.*
- Procrastination—*If I can't do this perfectly the very first time, I won't do it at all.*

I have personally struggled with each of these demons. I'm not alone. If you let doubt fester, it turns into Medusa with a head of writhing serpents and turns you to stone. Let's examine these stumbling blocks, dispel limiting beliefs, and slay Medusa.

CAN STRUGGLE BUILD SUPERPOWERS?

The myth is that people succeed *in spite of* hardship. People say things such as:

- *In spite of* the fact that he grew up in foster homes, Wayne Dyer inspired millions of people as an author and speaker.
- Oprah Winfrey became a billionaire and one of the most influential people in the world—*in spite of* her traumatic and impoverished childhood.
- *In spite of* the cracked foundation of his youth, David Goggins became a Navy SEAL.

What if our thinking is backward? What if these people achieved their success not *in spite of*—but *because of*—the challenges they faced? What if loss triggers a state change and a new perspective? What if loss can be transformed into leadership?

Inspired by David Goggins, an ultramarathon runner, my son Yale Winter started jogging recently. Yale urged me to check out Goggins' Instagram feed. When I did so, I was struck by Goggins' handsome, chiseled features, and his strong, lean body as he jogged along the beach, belting out a galvanizing message to "stay hard!"

But Goggins was not always such an impressive human being. Goggins grew up with what he called "a cracked foundation." His father was an abusive alcoholic. Both he and his mother suffered mental and physical abuse. So his mother had a "cracked foundation," too. Goggins had no one to show him the ropes, show him the way.

Things went from bad to worse when his family moved to a small town in Indiana with only five other black families, so you can imagine the prejudice and racial slurs. He had a learning disability and cheated to get through school, further eroding his self-worth. He developed social anxiety and a stutter. His foundation developed more cracks. No one was there to help him, and he realized he had to figure things out by himself.

"What made me who I am today is that cracked foundation—and not liking it. So I had to learn how to mend that cracked foundation alone," said Goggins. "I had to develop mental toughness. But to me, mental toughness was not enough. I had to really develop a calloused mind."

He decided to become his own hero. "I had a victim mentality —I was a victim. Everybody messed my life up, my Dad, society, my Mom," said Goggins. "I was dealt a bad hand. So I developed a way to get over the victim mentality. And it was through callousing my mind. **I was literally callousing over the victim mentally through outworking all my faults.**"

His struggle and determination to overcome adversity resulted in him "callousing over the victim mentally." In other words, he rewired his brain. He built layers of myelin and laid down broadband.

As a result of retraining his mind and claiming his new, heroic identity, he transformed his body and his life. He quit his dead-end job spraying for cockroaches, lost over 100 pounds in 90 days, and was accepted into the elite Navy SEAL training. He survived the intense training (including three hell weeks). His body broke down, but his mind did not. Now a retired Navy SEAL, Goggins is one of the world's top ultra-endurance athletes and has earned the reputation as the world's toughest man.

"You have to be willing to suffer to get to the other side," said Goggins, author of *Can't Hurt Me: Master Your Mind and Defy the Odds.*

What if David Goggins did not become a Navy SEAL and the world's toughest man *in spite of* the cracked foundation of his childhood—*but because of it*, and his struggle to overcome it?

THE SURPRISING VALUE OF STRUGGLE

Talent is grown through three things: intense desire, deep practice, and training/coaching. Fierce desire fuels deep work. A primal state of focus where the stakes are high, it really matters, and we're focused, attentive—even desperate—sets up ideal conditions for the kind of effort that builds skill. In contrast, fond wishes do not. Working outside your comfort zone grows myelin and creates super-highways in the brain.

"Struggle is not optional—it's neurologically required," wrote Coyle in *The Talent Code*. "Deep practice is built on a paradox: struggling in certain targeted ways—operating at the edges of your ability, where you make mistakes—makes you smarter. Or to put it a slightly different way, experiences where you're forced to slow down, make errors, and correct them—as you would if you were walking up an ice-covered hill, slipping and stumbling as you go—end up making you swift and strong without you realizing it."

Every time we struggle to live up to our full potential, we are slowly installing broadband in our circuitry. As we work to triumph over adversity, we build skill and mastery.

"We think of effortless performance as desirable, but it's really a terrible way to learn," said Robert Bjork, UCLA chair of psychology. "Things that appear to be obstacles turn out to be desirable in the long haul."

Most people know that trauma can trigger PTSD (post-traumatic stress disorder). But few are aware that it can also trigger **post-traumatic growth**.

Leaders in the field of posttraumatic growth, Richard G. Tedeschi and Lawrence G. Calhoun, authors of *Posttraumatic Growth in Clinical Practice* wrote, "Growth, however, does not occur as a direct result of trauma. It is the individual's struggle with the new reality in the aftermath of trauma that is critical in determining the extent to which posttraumatic growth occurs."

Trauma is like an earthquake. It is as if your life was a brick house, and your house has collapsed, bricks strewn everywhere. You have a choice: despair or rebuild. The labor of rebuilding fosters growth.

Personal distress and growth coexist. Support makes a world of difference during this vulnerable time. As I know from coaching clients through life-altering events, the right question at the right time can open up empowering new possibilities and result in an adaptive, expansive response—rather than a maladaptive, shrinking reaction.

In my case, it was not the death of my husband that created posttraumatic growth. Instead, it was my battle to survive, rebuild, and discover the meaning of my life that created growth. I'm not grateful that my husband died—but I am thankful for the consciousness, grit, and empathy I developed as a result.

Ralph Waldo Emerson wrote, "The death of a dear friend, wife, brother, lover, which seemed nothing but privation, somewhat later assumes the aspect of a guide or genius; for it commonly operates revolutions in our way of life."

CRACKS LET THE LIGHT IN

Dr. Martin Seligman is the past president of the American Psychological Association and the author of several books on positive psychology, including *Authentic Happiness* and *Flourish*. He studied 1,700 people who had experienced the worst things that can happen in a person's lifetime: torture, death of a child, rape, grave illness, imprisonment, and so on.

Seligman wrote, "To our surprise, individuals who'd experienced one awful event had more intense strengths (and therefore higher well-being) than individuals who had none. Individuals who'd been through two awful events were stronger than individuals who had one, and individuals who had three—raped, tortured, and held captive for example—were stronger than those who had two."

That is the exact opposite of what we expect! It appears that these awful events triggered posttraumatic growth, and people changed in positive ways. Struggle builds strength in the gym and in life.

Trauma, setbacks, and grief challenge us to change and grow. When death brushes by, we face our own mortality. Confronted by the gap between our values and the way we spend each day, we shift. We recalibrate. To build a more meaningful life, people change direction.

People can breakdown—or breakthrough. Rather than being permanently scarred by awful events, people can gain a rare new perspective. By definition, leaders provide a fresh or uncommon worldview to their followers.

Extreme events that trigger a limit experience are not the exception for leaders, but rather the norm. (A limit experience is one where that your worldview breaks, your ego is shattered, and a new identity emerges like a Phoenix rising from the ashes.) Loss, trauma, and other awful events create enormous pressure, which can turn ordinary people into extraordinary leaders—just as pressure turns common carbon into a diamond.

Loss can—and does—launch leaders.

"There is a crack, a crack in everything, That's how the light gets in," wrote Leonard Cohen, the legendary Canadian singer, and poet.

He elaborated, "This is not the place where you make things perfect, neither in your marriage, nor in your work, nor anything, nor your love of God, nor your love of family or country. The thing is imperfect. And worse, there is a crack in everything that you can put together: physical objects, mental objects, constructions of any kind. But that's where the light gets in, and that's where the resurrection is and that's where the return is, that's where the repentance is. It is with the confrontation, with the brokenness of things."

WHO MAKES HISTORY?

What doesn't kill you makes you stronger. Is that true?

How can we scientifically measure the impact of a significant loss? One possibility is to consider losses that are unambiguous, such as the early death of a parent.

Is the loss of a parent at an early age crippling? Or can loss trigger creative genius? I had more than a casual interest in these questions as my son was only four years old when his father died. How would that impact his future?

A clinical psychologist named Martin Eisenstadt theorized that the loss of a parent at an early age was related to the development of genius. In the 1970s, to test his theory, he tracked every person eminent enough to warrant a half-page long entry in the *Encyclopaedia Britannica*. He traced the parental history of these 573 subjects, which ranged from Michelangelo to John F. Kennedy.

Early parent loss was shockingly common within this accomplished group. Scientists and artists on the parent-loss list include Newton (father, before birth), Copernicus (father, 10), Darwin (mother, 8), Dante (mother, 6), Michelangelo (mother, 6), Bach (mother and father, 9), Keats (father, 8, mother, 14), Handle (father, 11), Dostoyevsky (mother, 15), Byron (father, 3), Emerson (father, 8), Charlotte, Emily, and Anne Brontë (mother, at 5, 3, and 1 respectively), Melville (father, 12), Wordsworth (mother, 7, father 13), Nietzsche (father, 4), Twain (father, 11).

Political leaders who lost a parent in their youth or childhood include Washington (father, 11), Jefferson (father, 14), Lincoln (mother, 9), Gandhi (father, 15), Julius Caesar (father, 15), and fifteen British prime ministers. These prominent leaders in their respective fields had a disproportionately high ratio of early parent loss. On average, the distinguished group lost their first parent at the age of 13.9, compared with 19.6 for the control group. The incidence of parent loss amongst British prime ministers was twice as high as for their peers.

US President Bill Clinton's father died when he was an infant (and Barack Obama essentially lost his father at the age of two, when his father left the family).

Updating this list, courtesy of Coyle's outstanding book *The Talent Code*, here are a few more stars who lost a parent before the age of eighteen:

- **Comedy**: Steve Allen, Lucille Ball, Mel Brooks, Drew Carey, Stephen Colbert, Charlie Chaplin, Billy Crystal, Eddie Murphy, Rosie O'Donnell, Martin Short, Red Skelton, Tom and Dick Smothers, Tracy Ullman.
- **Music**: Louis Armstrong, Tony Bennett, Bono, 50 Cents, Aretha Franklin, Robert Goulet, Jimi Hendrix, John Lennon, Madonna, Paul McCartney.
- **Movies:** Cate Blanchett, Orlando Bloom, Mia Farrow, Jane Fonda, Daniel Day-Lewis, Sir Ian McKellen, Robert Redford, Julia Roberts, Martin Sheen, Barbara Streisand, Charlize Theron, Billy Bob Thornton, James Woods.
- **Note:** This list does not include those who lost a parent due to divorce, disease, abuse, or abandonment. Nor does it include people struggling with other challenges, such as Goggins, Oprah, and Branson fought to overcome.

Why could the loss of a parent stimulate rather than stunt growth? People may react with inferiority or industry. They can retreat, feeling defeated or inferior—or attack and work hard. The loss itself does not produce growth—but the fierce struggle to overcome adversity does.

Eisenstadt summed it up as a "springboard of immense compensatory energy." Losing a parent at a young age can become a motivational trigger. It is a primal cue: you are in danger. It trips the "survival of the fittest" trigger and can unleash massive action.

In his book *Origins of Genius*, Dean Keith Simonton wrote that the loss of a parent could "nurture the development of a personality robust enough to overcome the many obstacles and frustrations standing in the way of achievement."

Simonton notes that other kinds of adverse experiences may sometimes enhance genius. For example, eminent creators seem disproportionately handicapped by physical challenges such as affected Thomas Edison, Aldous Huxley, Rudyard Kipling, and Stevie Wonder.

In *Greatness: Who Makes History and Why* Simonton wrote, "An inspection of the lives of notables such as Keats, Swift, and Thackeray showed that 55% lost a parent before age 15. Another study found that the incidence of orphanhood for recipients of the Nobel Prize for literature was over eight times higher than that for the Nobel Prize for physics."

"Ten thousand hours is the magic number for greatness," wrote Malcolm Gladwell in *Outliers* (based on the work of Anders Ericsson). In other words, mastery requires putting in the time and effort to learn and is not just based on innate talent.

Gladwell popularized the 10,000-Hour Rule, and while some may quibble about the exact number of hours, no one debates that practice is needed to master a new skill. Losing a parent can change a person's world view. It could unleash the energy and dedication required for mastery.

Loss can and *does* launch leaders. Leaders dig deep and overcome incredible challenges—that is the quintessential hero's journey.

The dictionary defines a hero as "a person noted for courageous acts or nobility of character."

In *The Hero with a Thousand Faces*, Joseph Campbell summarized the hero's journey: "A hero ventures forth from the world of common day into a region of supernatural wonder: fabulous forces are there encountered and a decisive victory is won: the hero comes back from this mysterious adventure with the power to bestow boons on his fellow man."

Like David Goggins, you can claim the path of the hero. As Goggins demonstrated, struggle can build superpowers.

The Imposter Syndrome

EVEN THE BEST and brightest suffer from feeling like imposters. Perhaps especially the best and brightest. In his commencement address *This Is Water*, David Foster Wallace said, "Everybody worships. The only choice we get is what to worship.... Worship your intellect, being seen as smart, you will end up feeling stupid, a fraud, always on the verge of being found out."

Can you guess who called himself an "involuntary swindler" in his twilight years? One of the most highly respected minds of all time—Albert Einstein! If Albert Einstein suffered from feelings of inadequacy, clearly achieving more is not the antidote to the Imposter Syndrome.

High achieving women are particularly susceptible to the Imposter Syndrome, according to a study published by the American Psychological Association. Pauline Clance and Suzanne Imes wrote, "Despite outstanding academic and professional accomplishments, women who experience the impostor phenomenon persist in believing that they are really not bright and have fooled anyone who thinks otherwise."

Vulnerability expert Brené Brown, the author of *Daring Greatly* wrote, "The irony is that we attempt to disown our difficult stories to appear more whole or more acceptable, but our wholeness—even our whole-heartedness—actually depends on the integration of all our experiences, including the falls."

Brené Brown had to bolster her own resolve as she stepped into the spotlight. She found these words from US President Theodore Roosevelt helpful:

> *"It is not the critic who counts; not the man who points out how the strong man stumbles, or where the doer of deeds could have done them better. The credit belongs to the man who is actually in the arena, whose face is marred by dust and sweat and blood; who strives valiantly; who errs, who comes short again and again, because there is no effort without error and shortcoming; but who does actually strive to do the deeds; who knows great enthusiasms, the great devotions; who spends himself in a worthy cause; who at the best knows in the end the triumph of high achievement, and who at the worst, if he fails, at least fails while daring greatly, so that his place shall never be with those cold and timid souls who neither know victory nor defeat."*
>
> ~ THEODORE ROOSEVELT ~

Mindset

STANFORD PSYCHOLOGY PROFESSOR Carol Dweck, author of *Mindset: The New Psychology of Success*, discovered the one personality trait that was the springboard for a lifetime of achievement. This one trait made people more successful, creative and fulfilled.

Mindset governs the way we think about virtually every aspect of our lives. Dweck ascertained that people have either a "fixed mindset" or a "growth mindset." People with a fixed mindset believe that their character, intelligence, and creative potential are fixed. Striving for success and avoiding failure at all costs becomes a way of life.

On the other hand, people with a growth mindset love learning and expect that they can master new skills, provided they put in the time and effort.

If you have a fixed mindset, you will see setbacks as failure. Getting fired. Getting rejected. Getting a bad grade, getting passed over for promotion. Any of these setbacks are blows to your self-worth as they mean you are not talented.

In contrast, if you have a growth mindset, you will see failure as not learning, not growing, not stretching to achieve your goals. It means you're not fulfilling your potential. You are less concerned about the opinions of others. You know that effort will build your skill and capacity.

So which mindset do you think promotes creativity, resilience, and perseverance? Which mindset will produce greater capabilities over a lifetime? If you said a growth mindset, you'd be right.

When she first learned about mindset, Dweck was confronted by all the ways that she had a fixed mindset herself. I had the same uncomfortable awareness. For example, I realized thinking that I'm not technical is a fixed mindset. The truth is, I simply haven't spent enough time to learn how to code.

The good news is that you can upgrade a fixed mindset to a growth mindset with six magic words.

SIX MAGIC WORDS

Dweck shared an experiment that revealed the powerful impact of coaching. The goal was to see how a single sentence of praise influenced performance and effort, and what kind of praise was most effective.

She conducted a series of experiments in New York with four hundred fifth graders. First, each child was given a test comprised of easy puzzles. Afterwards, the children were each informed of their score, followed by a single sentence of praise. Half the kids were praised for their effort *("You must have worked really hard")* while the other half were praised for their intelligence *("You must be smart at this")*.

Then the kids were tested again, but this time they were offered a choice between a harder test and an easier test. A full ninety percent of the kids who'd been praised for their effort chose the harder test. In contrast, most of the kids who were praised for their intelligence chose the easy test. Why?

Dweck wrote, "When we praise kids for their intelligence, we tell them that's the name of the game: Look smart, don't risk making mistakes."

The third level of tests was even more challenging, and none of the kids scored well. But the kids praised for their intelligence hated the experiment. In contrast, the kids praised for their effort were fully engaged, tried various solutions, and enjoyed the challenge. As the final step, the kids were once again given easy puzzles—the same level of difficulty as the initial test.

The results were shocking. Dweck was so surprised that she reran the study five times to confirm the findings. The praised-for-effort group improved their initial score by 30%, while the praised-for-smart group's score declined by 20%. **Six short words had caused the ratings to differ by 50%!** Acknowledging effort produces far better results than ego-stroking empty praise.

A growth mindset appears to act as an anti-depressant, as well. College students often get depressed in February as exams pile up, and winter drags on. Students with a fixed mindset let things slide more and more as their emotions cratered. They didn't study as much as needed, failed to hand in their assignments on time, and didn't keep up with their chores.

Growth mindset students also got depressed. But they responded in a completely different way. The *more* depressed the growth mindset students were, the *more* action they took to confront their problems, the *more* they made sure to keep up with their homework, and the *more* they kept up with their lives.

A fixed mindset sabotages effort and robs otherwise smart and talented people of their coping resources. In contrast, growth mindset people believe that their skills can be enhanced and developed.

The way to overcome the Imposter Syndrome is to choose a growth mindset and see "mistakes" as growth opportunities.

As the German proverb states, "You will become clever through your mistakes."

Procrastination

PROCRASTINATION AND PERFECTIONISM go hand in hand. Seth Godin wrote, "The tyranny of perfect: Perfect closes the door. It asserts that we are done, that this is the best we can do. Worse, perfect forbids us to try. To seek perfection and not reach it is a failure. The possibility of better: Better opens the door. Better challenges us to see what's there and begs us to imagine how we could improve on that. Better invites us in and gives us a chance to seek dramatic improvement on behalf of those we seek to serve."

Procrastination sabotages success while cloaking the real game we are playing. We lie to others—and ourselves. We say we will do it later—when we have more time, more money, more success, more clarity, more data.

Procrastination is a threat response. It's the "freeze" in "fight, flight, or freeze." Prey freeze, like rabbits stock-still in the wheat-colored field, hoping the mountain lion will not spot them. But you are not prey, and if fear makes you freeze, your croc brain has hijacked your mind.

HOW TO MAKE GOOD DECISIONS

Here's how the most-successful entrepreneur in the world makes decisions. In his *2016 Letter to Shareholders*, Jeff Bezos, founder, and CEO of Amazon wrote:

"The senior team at Amazon is determined to keep our decision-making velocity high. Speed matters in business—plus a high-velocity decision-making environment is more fun too. We don't know all the answers, but here are some thoughts.

"First, never use a one-size-fits-all decision-making process. Many decisions are reversible, two-way doors. Those decisions can use a light-weight process. For those, so what if you're wrong? I wrote about this in more detail in last year's letter.

"Second, most decisions should probably be made with somewhere around 70% of the information you wish you had. If you wait for 90%, in most cases, you're probably being slow. Plus, either way, you need to be good at quickly recognizing and correcting bad decisions. If you're good at course correcting, being wrong may be less costly than you think, whereas being slow is going to be expensive for sure.

"Third, use the phrase 'disagree and commit.' This phrase will save a lot of time. If you have conviction on a particular direction, even though there's no consensus, it's helpful to say, 'Look, I know we disagree on this, but will you gamble with me on it? Disagree and commit?' By the time you're at this point, no one can know the answer for sure, and you'll probably get a quick yes."

To recap the wisdom of the richest man in the world (currently estimated at 110 billion), Jeff Bezos recommends:

- Speed matters—decide quickly
- Understand—most decisions are reversible
- Decide with 70% of the information you wish you had
- Disagree and commit
- So what if you're wrong? Course correct

Bezos is not alone in his views. Geoff Smart and Randy Street and their team from the University of Chicago analyzed data from over three hundred interviews with CEOs who led companies backed by private equity from 2000 to 2005. They then matched the CEO character traits with actual financial performance and discovered that CEOs who made decisions slowly after consulting others and getting more data were successful most of the time (57%).

On the other hand, fast and focused decision-making CEOs were successful 100% of the time—almost double the success rate of the ponderous decision-makers. For example, one such "Cheetah CEO" produced an impressive growth of 3,500%, increasing the stock price from $4 to $142 in just five years.

Is Bezos right about taking action without reaching a consensus? Absolutely. Self-made billionaire Ray Dalio agrees with Bezos:

"To make money in the markets, one needs to be an independent thinker who bets against the consensus and is right. That's because the consensus view is baked into the price.... To be a successful entrepreneur, the same is true: One also has to be an independent thinker who bets against the consensus," wrote Ray Dalio in *Principles.*

The founder of the hedge fund Bridgewater, Dalio was named the "Steve Jobs of Investing" by *WIRED* magazine and one of the 100 Most Influential People by *TIME* magazine. In 2019 his estimated net worth was $18 billion. Not as much as Bezos, whose net worth in 2019 was estimated at $111 billion, but then Bezos is the richest man alive, whereas Dalio is merely in the top 100.

Bezos and Dalio agree—consensus kills profit. Think of the greatest ideas of the past decade—like Uber or Airbnb. Most people were dubious. If everyone likes the idea, you will have a lot of competition.

All of the value lies in the surprise.

HOW TO BANISH FEAR

Leaders need to manage their fear and doubt. To be successful, entrepreneurs and investors need to steel their nerves to think independently and bet against the consensus. Facing fears squarely helps people avoid paralyzing procrastination.

"Named must your fear be before banish it you can," Yoda advised young Luke Skywalker in *Star Wars*.

"Fear-setting has produced my biggest business and personal successes, as well as repeatedly helped me to avoid catastrophic mistakes," said Tim Ferriss in his 2017 TED talk *Why You Should Define Your Fears Instead of Your Goals*.

Most people overlook the costs of NOT taking action. That is a big mistake. Not doing anything is a decision. Look at what inaction costs. If things stay the same, how will you feel about your life in a year or two? Who will you become in a decade if you don't pursue the things that interest you?

Ferriss was working insane hours but had little to show for it. His girlfriend left. Something had to change. He wanted to take a break but was afraid of catastrophic consequences. Using fear-setting, Ferriss saw that the worst-case scenario was modest and recoverable, whereas the upside was impressive and long-term.

So he took a sabbatical. As he traveled around Europe, he discovered ways to outsource tasks related to his business. He turned those discoveries into *The Four-Hour Workweek*, which catapulted him from an unknown, struggling entrepreneur to a famous, prosperous author and popular podcast host. Facing his fears produced long-term benefits beyond his wildest dreams.

Facing my own fears and examining the worst-case scenarios of *both* action and inaction prompted me to make sweeping changes in my life and business in 2014.

Feeling miserable after a breakup, I started drinking too much. I threw myself into my work, but that just made my life increasingly out of balance and unrewarding. I was headed towards burnout and maybe bankruptcy, too. Something had to change before I had a physical, mental, or financial breakdown. But what?

I realized the thought "It's too late" was casting a resigned shadow over all my decisions. Too late to get an MBA, too late to find love again, too late to start a new business, too late to ... you-name-it.

I asked myself, "Is that true? Is it too late?" and discovered that I had unwittingly installed an actuarial table in my head. But an actuarial table is a trailing indicator based on historical *statistical averages*—it is not an accurate *future* prediction for any one specific *individual.*

Exponential advances in medicine make it reasonable to assume that actuarial tables underestimate lifespan. For example, advances in genome sequencing are happening at an exponential rate surpassing Moore's law, creating new possibilities for biohacking.

In a 2012 interview on PBS *Newshour*, respected futurist Ray Kurzweil said, "We will get to a point 15 years from now where, according to my models, we will be adding more than a year every year to your remaining life expectancy, where the sands of time are running in rather than running out, where your remaining life expectancy actually stretches out as time goes by."

Dan Sullivan, many years my senior, intends to live to 156, Dave Asprey to 180, and Peter Diamandis to 600!

This information helped refute my gloomy thought, "It's too late," but the clincher was that I was surely hastening my own expiry date and creating a self-fulfilling prophesy by allowing the thought "It's too late" to take root in my mind. I had to uproot that noxious weed!

I had been flirting with the idea of getting my MBA for years, but it hadn't seemed urgent. "If not now, when?" prompted me to take action. I put my business on hold and moved to Italy to take my MBA in 2014-15. And that changed everything, creating a fresh new chapter.

Shrink fear by facing reality. Answer these questions:

1. Define your nightmare—what is the worst that could happen if you wrote a book, took a year off in Europe, or pursued your fondest dream?
2. If everything went horribly wrong, what steps could you take to repair the damage?
3. If your business or career ended today, what would you do to get things under financial control?
4. What are you putting off out of fear? Is the fear life-threatening…or merely ego-threatening?
5. What is it costing you to postpone taking action? Where will you be 10 years from now if you don't take action?
6. What are the likely benefits and outcomes in 10 weeks, 10 months, and 10 years if you took action?
7. What if you lived to be 100 or 150? Would you change course?
8. How does your expectation of the length of your life impact your choices, engagement, health, relationships—and actual life expectancy?

9. What if you get beyond the age of interest and "later" turns into "never"? What will you regret not doing?
10. Who else will benefit from your bold choices?
11. Who else will suffer from your fearful choices?
12. If not now, when? What are you waiting for?

How to Avoid Regret

"BEGIN WITH THE end in mind," recommends Steven Covey, the author of *Seven Habits of Highly Effective People*. So, begin with the end of your life in mind. Imagine your own funeral. Who would be there? How many lives have you touched? Who will miss you when you're gone?

Who would you need to be to have 1,000 people attend your final *bon voyage* party—your celebration of life? The answer will reveal how each one of us could build a more meaningful life, starting today. To missed when you die, you do **not** need to be:

- Thin
- Beautiful
- Rich
- Powerful
- Famous
- Married to Someone Rich, Powerful, or Famous
- An Ivy-League Graduate
- A Social Media Influencer
- Listed in "Who's Who"
- An elected Leader

Many people spend the bulk of their time chasing things on the above list. How about you?

Looking for role models, I'm inspired by two examples: my niece, Mikayla Martin, who died in 2019 at the age of 22, and R. Buckminster Fuller, who died in 1983 at the age of 87. At a glance, they could not be more different. Mikayla was a young, female athlete and Buckminster was an old, male engineer. Yet they both impacted many people and, as a result, had "standing room only" at their final *bon voyage* party.

They were missed, in part, because they were:

- Fully engaged in life
- Determined
- Caring
- Connected
- A life-long learner
- Bold
- Focused on meaning, rather than money
- An author
- Goal-oriented
- A servant Leader

Both Martin and Fuller had an amazing zest for life. Fuller often spoke 100 times a year, sharing his vision of a world that works for everyone. He wrote over two dozen books. He kept up a vigorous pace, with his last speaking engagement two weeks before he died at the age of 88.

Although she was only 22 when she died, Martin had a full life worth celebrating. She was a member of the Canadian National Ski Cross team and was the World Junior Champion in 2018.

She studied stock trading with my brother, Calvin Winter, PhD, and co-authored a book with him.

Like Fuller, she kept up a vigorous pace. In the three months before her death, she attended two ski training camps; medaled in two ski cross races in Australia; got her full motorcycle license; earned her open water SCUBA certification; went diving on the Great Barrier Reef; climbed the Chief in under 30 minutes; and organized a sunset fondue dinner at Elfin Lakes with her parents.

Time is our most precious resource. Most people spend a lot of time thinking about money. Money is a renewable resource. Currency flows infinitely.

But your breath will not continue to flow forever. Your body is mortal. We never know how much time we have. It is vital to play full out, make every day count. Once a day is wasted, you can never get it back. Ever.

Grief is a powerful medicine that immunizes us from a life half-lived. It builds antibodies of purpose, meaning, character, clarity, grit, and resilience.

TOP 5 DEATHBED REGRETS

In her book *The Top Five Regrets of the Dying* palliative care nurse Bronnie Ware shares the most common regrets:

- I wish I had lived a life true to my dreams, instead of what others expected of me.
- I wish I hadn't worked so hard.
- I wish I had stayed in touch with my friends.
- I wish I had let myself be happier.
- I wish I'd had the courage to express my true self.

When death or disaster brushes close by, it transports us to our own deathbed in our mind's eye. That can fuel change.

To avoid regret, ask yourself these questions:

- How can I let go of the expectations of others, and live a life true to myself and my own dreams?
- How can I create a life of meaning and purpose?
- How can I build better relationships with friends and family?
- How can I design my life so that I'm happy and flourishing?
- How can I express my true self more fully, and not die with my music inside me?

Your answers to the above questions can reshape your life.

Ware shared, "When people realize that their life is almost over and look back clearly on it, it is easy to see how many dreams have gone unfulfilled. Most people had not honored even a half of their dreams and had to die knowing that it was due to choices they had made, or not made. Health brings a freedom very few realize until they no longer have it."

WHAT FOOTPRINTS WOULD YOU LEAVE?

- How would you like to be remembered?
- Who would you like to influence and inspire?
- What legacy would you like to leave?

"Pursue what is meaningful—not what is expedient."
~ Jordan Peterson ~

10 YOUR TURN

"What To Do When It's Your Turn
(And It's Always Your Turn)"
~ Seth Godin ~

WHAT'S THE WORST ADVICE YOU EVER RECEIVED?

In *David Goggins Reveals How to Master Your Mind*, podcast host Rob Moore asked, "What's the worst advice you ever received?"

David Goggins replied, "The worst advice I ever received was from an agent. He said, 'If you self-publish your book you will sell five thousand copies—if you do this on your own, no one will buy this book.'"

After finding a writer to capture his words and stories, Goggins self-published his book *Can't Hurt Me: Master Your Mind and Defy the Odds*. Seven months later, in June of 2019, he had sold one million copies of his book and 650,000 copies of his audiobook. If he had listened to the agent and gone with the traditional, archaic publishing model, he would have forfeited about $20 million.

But that's not the reason Goggins chose to self-publish. He did not want to have to ask the publisher—or anyone—for permission to share his life story his way. Famous for having learned how to master his mind, life, and body, Goggins was not about to let someone else be the master of his speaking and publishing business.

Breaking with tradition once again, Goggins created a revolutionary new format for his audiobook, blending spontaneous podcast-style commentary with his manuscript being read aloud by Adam. This new format captured the raw, spontaneous, conversational energy that people love in podcast interviews and added that value to his audiobook. As a result, his loyal fans scooped up both the book and the audiobook.

Thinking Is A Multiplier

THINKING IS A multiplier. Everything is twice created. The idea comes first. You know this to be true. For example, the blueprint comes before the house is built.

Ideas are one of the few valuable things you can give away and still keep. For example, a blueprint can be used to build many houses. Due to the network effect, an idea that is freely given away often increases in value. For example, one person using Facebook is not as valuable as a million people adopting and using Facebook.

There are no neutral thoughts. Every thought creates. There is no such thing as an "idle thought."

A Course in Miracles states: "Everything you see is the result of your thoughts. There is no exception to this fact. Thoughts are not big nor little; powerful or weak. They are merely true or false. ... Every thought you have contributes to truth or illusion; it either extends the truth or multiplies illusions. Every thought you have brings either peace or war, either love or fear. A neutral result is impossible because a neutral thought is impossible."

Leaders engage in a war of words that can build—or sabotage—humanity's social, economic, and political future.

As I write this in the fall of 2019, Jordan Peterson's message has gone viral. One man's thinking about the importance of responsibility, cleaning up your room, and free speech has now reached millions of people. Interviews with him about his new book *12 Rules for Life: An Antidote to Chaos* have triggered many conversations far beyond the campus of the University of Toronto, where Peterson teaches.

For the first time in history, ideas can be transmitted to millions of people almost instantly—within a matter of days—thanks to the internet. Influencers can reach their audience directly, without their ideas being diluted, filtered, or delayed by a third party with a different agenda—such as big business, the media, or government.

A media-savvy author like Jordan Peterson leverages speaking with the printed word. A speaker can transmit ideas and emotions and sync brain waves with the audience through mirror neurons. Videos have the unique qualities of fidelity and speed.

On the other hand, books possess the valuable virtue of fidelity over time and space. Videos are like a blooming rose that quickly drops its dewy petals. Books, on the other hand, are like a rose bulb that can be planted years later and continents away and will blossom when fertilized by the reader's attention.

Radical Reading, Writing & Reflecting

TO BUILD YOUR business, brand, and book, you need ideas. To generate a stream of ideas, tap into your inner wisdom, and improve your life, I recommend that you practice the 3 RR's—Radical Reading, Writing, and Reflecting. These habits will open up the idea floodgates, flush out anything damming the flow, and recharge your enthusiasm. At least, that has been my experience. Give these habits a try for ninety days and see what happens!

RADICAL WRITING

Radical Writing—each morning, write two pages without stopping, without curbing your insane monkey mind but rather capturing that chatter on the page. Write down your crazy ideas, confess your lust, admit your fantasies, divulge your deepest, darkest secrets. Did you dream? Write it down. Speculate on what your dream might mean. This is not writing that you will show anyone—it's radical. Hence, the name.

But this is your chance to get to know yourself and all the divergent personalities housed within your meat suit. We tend to suppress and reject our thoughts, the unacceptable outliers, giving them no space to be heard. But something is clamoring to be heard—sometimes there is genius waiting to be released like a genie, requiring only a little rubbing. In this case, you are not rubbing Aladdin's Lamp but rather rubbing your pen on the smooth paper of your journal.

Other times, there is a deep dissatisfaction that needs to be acknowledged. Expressing it on paper in your journal is far better than expressing it as a disease, or exploding in uncontrolled rage. Rage needs to be heard, too, and tuning in to places where your boundaries have been violated is the first step to establishing healthy boundaries—or getting the hell out of a toxic situation.

Acknowledging your deep yearning is essential to "recalculating" like a GPS and course correcting. Tuning into what's missing is far better than attempting to blot out that "still, small voice" with addictions—or worse. If the success or failure of your family, our planet, and all life upon it depended upon your actions, would you continue to live the way you are living?

RADICAL REFLECTION

Radical Reflection—read your Radical Writing every Sunday. Do you see some patterns emerging? Is some action or course correction called for? Is some decision-making principle emerging? Is something in your blind spot that requires action before it sabotages you, your business, your relationships, or your mental, physical, or spiritual health?

Are you working too hard? Are you lonely? Are you noticing addictions? Is your "croc brain" hijacking your best thinking repeatedly? When does that occur? Is your "pain body" getting triggered a lot? What triggers it? How could you restructure your day to avoid emotional potholes? What new habits would take your success from hopeful to likely to inevitable?

Notice patterns. For example, you might notice that you have a trough of energy and emotion at 5 pm and automatically reach for a glass of wine. Radical Review helped me observe this pattern in myself, and so I decided to stop drinking and go for a walk at the end of the day instead. You could realize, as I did, that it is vital to decide in advance what time you will stop work. You may discover that skipping lunch is a bad idea, or that, if your day starts at 5 am, you need to have dinner before 7 pm. You could discern that a glass of wine on an empty stomach is trouble and that your expectation that it will soothe your tangled emotions is not, in fact, reflected in reality.

Capture your insights and decisions. Then burn this week's pages (if desired). Keep track of your insights and decisions, obviously.

RADICAL READING

Radical Reading—90 minutes before you intend to go to bed, turn off all electronics—that's the radical part. Before you start kicking and screaming, know that the light from our electronic devices compromises sleep quality. Deep thinking requires at least ninety minutes of uninterrupted time. We tend to have ingrained habits of interruption when we are using Smartphones, tablets, or computers. The urge to check Instagram or Facebook tugs at your mind, even if you resist the temptation, and that sabotages flow. Micro-interruptions produce shallow thought. Deep thought is required to live up to your full potential.

I recommend that you read a physical softcover or hardcover book. I know, I know, I like reading on my iPad, too, and am in love with how many books I can take with me on a trip. If you absolutely must read on your device, put it on airplane mode. That's non-negotiable. Choose to learn from the best thinkers. Explore your areas of curiosity. Read literature, the classics, fiction, spiritual books, self-help books, how-to books, biographies, history, best-selling books in your field. I have recommended many excellent books on these pages, so you could start with one of those books. Read things outside your standard areas of interest. Creativity is cross-pollinating ideas, so read widely.

At the end of the day, review three things that you are grateful for and acknowledge your character traits that helped create people, situations, and things to appreciate. You can do this in bed if you wish, so it takes no extra time. As you fall asleep, ask one question that you would truly like your subconscious mind (or your higher self, or God, or the Universe—whatever aligns with your belief system) to answer. In the morning, write down the answer—or the dreams that may contain the answer—in your Radical Writing.

MEANINGFUL MORNINGS

Meaningful Mornings—start your day off right. Get up earlier. Don't press the snooze button. Train your body and brain to follow through on your decisions. Build mental strength, starting with getting up on time.

I love getting up at 5 am or earlier. I treasure the peaceful morning hours and quiet time to write and reflect.

Build resilience with a few minutes of deep breathing. One lovely approach is to breathe deeply, then bring your attention sequentially to Gratitude, Acceptance, Intention, and Nonjudgment, using Dr. Greg Hammer's method (for details, refer to his *GAIN Without Pain* series of books). I also recommend Dr. Andrew Weil's 4-7-8 breath process, especially if you are feeling anxious or overwhelmed (you can find it on YouTube). Or simply gaze at a single candle flame while breathing deeply for a few minutes. Use whatever deep breathing or meditative process you prefer. Then grab your journal and get started on Radical Writing!

I'd love to hear your insights and experience using Radical Writing, Radical Reflection, Radical Reading, and Meaningful Mornings. What did you notice as you started to listen more deeply to your inner wisdom? Did you decide to change the trajectory of your life, business, relationships, or health? Share your journey! www.ThoughtLeaderCommunity.com

A Book Is Like Telepathy

A BOOK IS like telepathy that time travels. A book is intimate, personal, and accessible. The reader may be many years—or many miles away from the author. A book is an idea virus, a seed, that can lay dormant and germinate whenever the book is opened and read. Books can travel the space-time continuum.

A book can change the trajectory of someone's life. I can still remember the day when I was nine years old, and I had to reach up on my tiptoes to reach for the last book in C. S. Lewis's Narnia series from where it sat on the shelf in my school library. I remember the mix of excitement and anticipatory grief. Another enchanting Narnia book to read!

But the very last one—after I read this one, there would be no more Narnia books for me to read. At that moment, I was struck with awe by the magical power of books. Through words alone, the author had cast a spell that materialized an entire fantasy world and took me there, mesmerized. I had an overwhelming feeling of reverence, and at that moment, I decided to become a writer and to do whatever it took to become the best writer I could be. And I've been writing and studying communication, ever since.

Amazingly, the very same author changed the trajectory of my life a second time. When I read C. S. Lewis's book *A Grief Observed*, I appreciated the raw honesty, and it helped me realize that I wasn't crazy, that grief was an intense, other-worldly experience for others, too. Grief was a world where the abnormal was normal.

I realized that my own diary of healing could benefit others and gathered the courage to follow C. S. Lewis's lead and be vulnerable and transparent. As a result, *From Heartbreak to Happiness: An Intimate Diary of Healing* was published, the Grief Coach Academy was birthed, and many people were helped through grief.

C. S. Lewis was dead before I read any of his books, yet he mentored me. He continues to inspire me to become a better writer. His writings carry his thoughts and ideas forward in time.

What thoughts and ideas would you like to send forward in time? What matters to you?

Your Massively Transformative Purpose

YOUR MASSIVELY TRANSFORMATIVE Purpose is your North Star, your fuel, your magnet. It will make you unstoppable. It will make you compelling. It will attract support from unexpected quarters. Your clear intention is the firm foundation upon which everything else is built.

AURORA WINTER

Your Massively Transformative Purpose (MTP) answers this question:

IF THE SUCCESS OR FAILURE OF OUR PLANET AND ALL LIFE UPON IT DEPENDED UPON YOUR ACTIONS, WHAT WOULD YOU DO?

Your purpose springs forth from the depth of your soul, fed by your unique life experiences. It is not like the decal of water lily, lacking depth, and glued on top of your life. Your purpose is like a real water lily, rooted in the mud of your life experiences, floating on the gently undulating lake of your consciousness, offering its sweet scent and captivating beauty generously to all.

You are unique, and your purpose is unique. You are the only person alive on planet Earth who can fulfill your MTP precisely as you will. Therefore, it is both your joy and your responsibility.

To help you connect with the whispers in your soul, write down a list of:

- 24 things that you are curious about
- 12 massive problems you would like to solve

Nodes of curiosity and surprising intersections provide clues to your unique MTP. Focusing on what you are curious about will increase flow. When you create your MTP this way, it hacks flow, according to Steven Kotler, one of the world's leading experts on the neuroscience of peak performance, and the author of *Stealing Fire*.

"Flow is defined as an optimal state of consciousness, a state where you feel your best and perform your best. More specifically, the term refers to those moments of rapt attention and total absorption, when you get so focused on the task at hand that everything else disappears. Action and awareness merge. Your sense of self vanishes. Your sense of time distorts (either, typically, speeds up, or, occasionally, slows down). And throughout, all aspects of performance, both mental and physical, go through the roof," wrote Kotler.

Flow makes work feel joyful and effortless—while it can also increase creativity and productivity by as much as 500%. In flow, you could work only on Monday and get as much done as you typically would working Monday, Tuesday, Wednesday, Thursday, and Friday! You don't want to miss out on that 5-to-1 leverage.

After you have a list of things you're curious about and problems you'd like to solve, define your Massively Transformative Purpose (MTP). A powerful MTP has a strong polarity. It is a magnet. It will repel and attract. Your tribe will say, "YES! I agree! How can I help?"

The rest of the world may think you are crazy, delusional, or an ego-maniac. Expect your perfectly-selected MTP to be challenged, scorned, or doubted by others. That is a sign you are on the right track. The words you choose to capture your intention are your shield and your sword. They create a boundary and demarcation of the area you have selected to protect, to heal, to champion. Your MTP will help you weather life's inevitable storms.

A perfect storm devastated Buckminster Fuller—he was expelled from Harvard, his business failed, he lost all his money. He lost the confidence of his friends and family, who had invested in his business. As if all of that was not bad enough, his baby daughter died.

Things looked hopeless. He had no money, no degree, no reputation, and no prospects. Fuller despaired, on the brink of committing suicide. But then he heard a voice that told him he did not have the right to end his life—his life did not belong to him. Fuller understood that he (and every other human being) belonged to the Universe. This revelation changed his life:

> *"So I vowed to keep myself alive, but only if I would never use me again just for me—each one of us is born of two, and we really belong to each other. I vowed to do my own thinking instead of trying to accommodate everyone else's opinions, credos, and theories. I vowed to apply my own inventory of experiences to the solving of problems that affect everyone on planet Earth."*
>
> ~ Buckminster Fuller ~

How does that strike you? Here is my reaction: "This moved me to tears. No one is coming to save us. No one is coming to save Mother Earth. It is up to us. We are all connected in the web of life. Each person can see and take action to solve the problem that is right in front of them, in their own area of enthusiasm and expertise, in their own family, neighborhood, or business. We have a worldwide web of information. What if we had a worldwide web of compassionate, caring, proactive leadership? What if we triggered a grass-roots movement independent of government or large, lumbering, self-serving corporations? We would be unstoppable!"

Fuller remained true to his purpose for the rest of his life. He demonstrated the enormous impact that one man without a degree or money can create. Devoted to creating "more with less," Fuller invented the geodesic dome, which made low-cost housing a reality. He was continually thinking of things to benefit humanity and wrote dozens of patents and books.

An engineer by training, Fuller stated that the most important thing is integrity, by which he meant to hold one's shape. A bridge that has integrity does not collapse in the wind. Your MTP will help you retain your shape and not be swayed by the opinions of others.

L. Steven Sieden shared some classic Fuller declarations and audience reactions in his book, *A Fuller View: Buckminster Fuller's Vision of Hope and Abundance for All.* This superb book influenced me to raise my standards, and I hope a taste of it will help you envision a bigger, bolder future.

"The most special thing about me is that I am an average man. I say that as a challenge to any limitation you may have accepted in your life."
~ BUCKMINSTER FULLER ~

Robert White shared how the above words impacted him, "My business success and lots of therapy had not been adequate to erase a history of feeling "less than." I felt I needed to stretch in order to get up to average, and here was one of my heroes saying firmly and sincerely that he was just that: average. ... Something shifted within me, and it has made all the difference in my life. Bucky stole my best excuse for being and doing less than my potential."

Have you been using a sense of not being "good enough" to avoid living up to your full potential?

"We are called to be architects of the future, not its victims. The challenge is to make the world work for 100% of humanity in the shortest possible time, with spontaneous cooperation, and without ecological damage or disadvantage to anyone."

~ Buckminster Fuller ~

What kind of future would you design?

"I live on Earth at present, and I don't know what I am. I know I am not a category. I am not a thing—a noun. I seem to be a verb, an evolutionary process—an integral function of Universe."

~ Buckminster Fuller ~

How can you take the right action?

"You have to decide whether you want to make money or make sense as the two are mutually exclusive."

~ Buckminster Fuller ~

Here, Fuller is talking about an error of thinking—chasing the SYMBOL of value—rather than VALUE itself. If you create value, the natural byproduct is wealth (unless you have a kink in your "receiving" hose). Giving and receiving occur simultaneously and define each other. If you idolize the symbol of wealth, your thinking is inaccurate. You may do things that don't make sense. You can't eat dollar bills. But producing true wealth makes sense.

Fuller was emphasizing the importance of intention. If you intend to make money and hoard it, your plans will not be backed by others (or by the principles of Nature), and you are likely to fail. On the other hand, if you intend to create value and contribute to others, that makes sense. Your plans will be supported, and you are likely to succeed. By putting his focus on projects that made sense, Fuller generated an annual income of over one million dollars in the 1950s. Understanding that Nature never hoards, he reinvested his income in other worthwhile projects that would help humanity thrive.

Making money is good, but meaningful work and meaningful relationships are far better. In *Principles*, Ray Dalio wrote, "Think about it: It's senseless to have making money as your goal as money has no intrinsic value—its value comes from what it can buy, and it can't buy everything. It's smarter to start with what you really want, which are your real goals, and then work back to what you need to attain them."

Money is a commodity, a tool to achieve your goals. What are your goals? How can you create real value?

"On the edge of a large ship's rudder is a miniature rudder called a trimtab. Moving that trimtab builds a low pressure which turns the rudder that steers the giant ship with almost no effort. In society, one individual can be a trimtab, making a major difference and changing the course of the gigantic ship of state. So I said, 'Call me Trimtab.'"

~ Buckminster Fuller ~

Fuller was a Trimtab. You can be one, too.

Now you are likely in a favorable frame of mind to create your own Massively Transformative Purpose (MTP). I recommend you take a few calming meditative breaths, then write your MTP. Share who or what you have decided to serve, to champion, to build. Write down how this will make the world (or your corner of it) a better place. Declare who you have decided to be in a series of "I am" statements. As an example, here is what I declared.

My Massively Transformative Purpose

To launch Thought Leaders who serve as independent leaders (or Trimtabs) in their own field of expertise and enthusiasm, with the overall result that we collectively raise the consciousness, playfulness, and prosperity of every life we touch, blessing humanity and Mother Earth. I am an alchemist who helps the architects of a better future transmute the heavy lead of setbacks, trauma, and grief into the gold of wisdom, compassion, and enlightenment.

I Am Statements

- *I am creating*
- *I am trusting*
- *I am a catalyst for miracles*
- *I am thriving*
- *I am connecting with creative, innovative, caring people*
- *I am launching Thought Leaders!*

Now it's your turn. I'd love to read your Massively Transformative Purpose and your "I am" declarations! Please share them here: www.ThoughtLeaderCommunity.com

YOUR MOONSHOT GOAL

Now that you are clear on your purpose, the next step is to create your Moonshot Goal. Step into a bigger vision for the global difference that you could make. What is your moonshot goal?

Creating a 25-year plan is beyond the scope of this book, but it is something I love to help my clients do. Here is a tip to get you started: think big, then 10× it. You are capable of much more than you think.

Build assets, such as your book, your business, and your brand. These assets can continue to provide value while you do something else, such as taking a year off to travel, launching another business, or writing another book.

I think it is a tragic waste of human potential that the best and brightest are typically so busy that their thoughts and life experience never get captured in a book.

If you can help others persevere in the face of obstacles, your message is worth sharing. If you can spare other people stress, grief, or tragic wrong turns, that's priceless. If you can help others love and accept themselves and others so they can build better relationships and a better life, that's important. If your expertise and experience can help others be healthier, happier, wealthier, your message is valuable.

Now it's your turn. I'd love to hear your Moonshot Goal! Why did you choose that goal? Who will it impact? Share your thoughts here www.ThoughtLeaderCommunity.com.

Conclusion: Leadership Matters More Than Ever

EVERY LEADER NEEDS the ability to communicate powerfully in both the written and spoken word.

In times of massive change, the future is vulnerable. Leadership is the rudder (or Trimtab) that keeps us going in the right direction. Our society is evolving at warp speed. Ideas are coming fast and furious, and the time delay between thinking and creating is shrinking. Change is happening at an exponential—not a linear—rate. There is more opportunity—and more danger.

Whether we create an adaptive, constructive future or a maladaptive, destructive future depends largely upon the thinking that prevails. Now is an important time for you to clarify, polish, and then broadcast ideas that will enhance the present and the future.

The Renaissance birthed many creative geniuses, including Michelangelo, Donatello, and Leonardo da Vinci due to the Apprentice model, where promising youth learned by modeling the work of Masters. Today, books, audios, and videos provide almost instant mentoring to anyone in the world with an internet connection and a smartphone. If you would like your best thinking to influence the future, now is the time to share your message!

Thinking is a multiplier. What thoughts will you multiply? What legacy will you leave? What Massively Transformative Purpose will you fulfill? What Moonshot Goal would you like to achieve?

Attention is our most limited and precious resource. Thought Leaders earn our trust and our attention. Blazing this trail are leaders such as Richard Branson, Tim Ferriss, Arianna Huffington, Ray Dalio, Sheryl Sandburg, David Goggins, Jeff Bezos, Steven Kotler, Oprah Winfrey, and Jordan Peterson.

It's never been more important—or more valuable—to step into the media spotlight as a Thought Leader due to exponential social, economic, and technological change.

SOCIAL CHANGE

People's attention spans are shrinking. People rely on shortcuts to decide if they should grant you any attention. Those shortcuts include authority and status. Authors are trusted experts with authority and status. Business moves at the speed of trust.

ECONOMIC CHANGE

There are more opportunities than ever before to become rich, thanks to exponential technological change. Platforms such as Paypal, Venmo, Yelp, AirBnb, eBay, and others have opened up larger markets and increased certainty and transaction speed.

In 2018, Amazon had almost half of the ecommerce market with revenue of $260 billion. A staggering 75% of Americans shop on Amazon most of the time. If your business involves some kind of expertise, you are missing out if you don't have a book showcasing that expertise on Amazon. People on Facebook are connecting, people on Google are searching, but people on Amazon are **buying**.

TECHNOLOGICAL CHANGE

Exponential technological change is creating new advantages everywhere, including in publishing and broadcasting. A new wave is rapidly replacing the old ways of doing business, and alert leaders and entrepreneurs are exploiting new opportunities.

Technological advances have made print-on-demand publishing and worldwide distribution widely available. Publishing is no longer restricted to the elite, but is for the people, by the people.

WRITING IS HARD

The only problem is—writing is as hard as ever. Fortunately, Thought Leaders can delegate the tedious details of creating, editing, publishing, and marketing their book.

A wordsmith wrangles words. A Thought Leader wrangles ideas. The author of a book is rightfully the person whose thoughts, expertise, and experiences it expresses.

Sir Winston Churchill dictated his thoughts and relied upon a team of ghostwriters, editors, and researchers to turn his spoken words into his written words. As a result, he was a prolific writer, influencing millions. Movie stars, politicians, and business tycoons take advantage of this solution, and you can, too.

REACHING THE MASSES

Entrepreneurs and leaders want to sell their innovative solutions to the mass market. But the majority distrust change—only 16% of any market is receptive to new ideas. As Geoffrey Moore explained, this presents the expensive and challenging problem of crossing the chasm that separates the Early Adopters from the lucrative Early Majority.

One proven way to bridge this gap and reach the mass market is to broadcast your ideas as a Thought Leader. People who have something valuable to say prove it by distilling and organizing their thoughts, expertise, and experiences into a book. The media craves clear, concise, compelling messages and energetic, engaging messengers. Media-trained authors can access media coverage, potentially worth millions of dollars in free advertising. People distrust advertising, but trust experts. Appearing as a guest expert is much more valuable than paid advertising.

New media outlets are springing up every day, eager for guest experts. Engaging guests can reach the masses without paying a dime for advertising. Appearing on podcasts and broadcasts can create a tipping point for you, your business, and your brand.

Becoming a media-savvy author is the recipe for a rapid rise to stardom that Jordan Peterson, Mel Robbins, and Hal Elrod used. David Goggins sold over a million copies of his self-published book in just seven months in 2019.

A book is an idea virus. A book can launch a startup or a movement. It can intimately influence people now—and for many years to come. To recap:

- Thought Leaders write books.
- Books build authority and expertise.
- Books are the key to free media coverage.
- Media-savvy leaders reach the masses as guest experts on podcasts and broadcasts.
- Trust is built, crossing the chasm.
- Ideas, products, and services reach the mass market.
- Books launch businesses and movements.

To win as an entrepreneur and Thought Leader, I recommend that you build and leverage:

- Your Million-Dollar Message
- Your Brand
- Your Spotlight
- Your Million Dollar Book
- Your Thought Leader Launch Blueprint
- Your Mentor
- Your Mastermind
- Your Legacy

We launch Thought Leaders, and we'd love to help you take the next steps. My team and I help leaders turn their ideas into books. We help leaders create solid business strategies and go-to-market plans. We provide media training so that you can step confidently into the spotlight, whether on TV or TED. We'd love to talk to you. Book a business breakthrough call here: www.BookCall.biz.

Our rapidly-changing world needs leaders more now than ever before. If not now, when?

It's your time. The world is waiting.

"I think everyone should write a book."
~ Richard Branson ~

Multiply Your ROI

GET YOUR FREE *Thought Leader Launch* starter library here: www.ThoughtLeaderLaunch.com.

In case you skipped it at the start of the book, these 10 steps will multiply the value you receive from reading this book.

1. Leaders have a big, bold vision. What problems would you like to solve? What are you curious about? Clarify the legacy you intend to leave and the impact you want to make. This becomes your North Star. *Leaders have a Massively Transformative Purpose.*

2. What is the next step that will help you fulfill your Massively Transformative Purpose? Leaders take bold actions. Take some action every day toward achieving your goals. *Leaders take action.*

3. Reading is a superpower. Books contain the expertise and experience of the most successful people alive today—and the wisdom of those who have been dead for hundreds of years. Reading is the fastest way to get new ideas. Books are a way to be privately mentored by people who have already achieved the goals that are on your vision board. The right idea at the right time can be a game-changer. *Leaders are readers.*

4. Doing everything by yourself is kryptonite. Leaders leverage their own strengths, and delegate the rest. They don't waste their time floundering to do everything by them-

selves. Leaders surround themselves with smart, capable, competent people who are aligned with their vision. *Leaders build teams.*

5. Leaders generate ideas which enhance their life, business, and the world. They replenish their creativity by taking the time to read, write, and reflect. Reflect on what you are learning and write it down. By writing it down, you cement your key takeaways. Writing is thinking. *Leaders read, write, and reflect.*

6. Share your insights with others. Share the #1 thing you learned—or were reminded of—by reading this book. Sharing multiplies value. Please post a brief book review on Amazon or your favorite bookstore. You will be encouraging me to continue writing, and helping others discover this book. Thank you! *Leaders generously help others.*

7. Embrace new habits for 90 days and watch your life, relationships, and business transform! Practice the habits explained in this book, including: Radical Reading, Radical Writing, Radical Reflection, Meaningful Mornings, and these Leadership Habits. Tiny actions, repeated daily, are transformative. *Leaders have daily success habits.*

8. Your brand is not a logo. Your brand is your story—and the stories of the value you created for your clients. Knowing that business moves at the speed of trust, leaders build trust. They make it easy for people to "know, like, and trust them." Leaders attract premium opportunities with a strong brand. Without a valuable brand, a product or service is a just a commodity—which means that the lowest price will win. *Leaders build their brand.*

9. Leaders look for new ways to add more value to their clients, coworkers, and community. They are open-minded, receptive, and innovative. *Leaders are curious.*

10. Leaders create impact. They leave the world a better place. They write books, give talks, and build businesses that make a meaningful difference. They share their expertise and experience, enriching the world. *Leaders leave a legacy.*

10 HABITS OF LEADERS: RECAP

1. Leaders have a Massively Transformative Purpose.
2. Leaders take action.
3. Leaders are readers.
4. Leaders build teams.
5. Leaders read, write, and reflect.
6. Leaders build their brand.
7. Leaders generously help others.
8. Leaders have daily success habits.
9. Leaders are curious.
10. Leaders leave a legacy.

Suggestion: Post this where you will see it every day. Small actions, repeated consistently, will transform your life, business, and leadership!

Free *Thought Leader Launch* starter library—available for a limited time. Get your bonuses here today:

WWW.THOUGHTLEADERLAUNCH.COM

PRAISE FOR AURORA AS A SPEAKER & TRAINER

"Saying that Aurora is a "good" speaker doesn't capture the magic that happened when Aurora was a guest speaker for my class. My students and I were fully engaged from the powerful and heartfelt presence she embodies. Aurora is a true professional, and I give her the highest recommendation as a speaker."

– **Mattie Clark**, Adjunct Lecturer, University of Iowa

"It was a powerful experience to have Aurora Winter as a speaker. She is a wonderful speaker and I would recommend her to any group without hesitation. She made my job easy!"

– **Marcia Sutton**, Human Resources Manager, Dole

"Aurora Winter is an incredible champion for startups and new technologies. If you're looking for someone to bolster your team with striking insights and boundless energy and passion, I highly recommend Aurora."

– **Tarrnie Williams**, CEO, Blueprint Reality

"Aurora is a terrific, dynamic speaker. She was a delight to work with. I have no hesitation recommending her."

– **Stephen Gregg**, Kaiser Permanente

"Aurora Winter and I crossed paths at a very interesting time in my career. My business evolved exponentially, and my team grew to more than 400 people. Aurora is a rock star, and I'm lucky to have her on my team!"

– **Jason Henneberry**, CEO, Tango Financial

"Aurora Winter is a very strategic, creative, innovative thinker. Aurora helped me leverage the success of my popular TEDx talk to grow my business, team, impact, and influence. If you're looking for a business coach to help you grow your business and grow personally and professionally, I highly recommend Aurora."

– **Louise Evans**, TEDx speaker,
author, entrepreneur

"A special thanks to Aurora Winter. She encouraged me to write my book during my sabbatical. Her "Thought Leader" program is incredibly well conceived and presented."

– **Greg Hammer, MD**, author,
GAIN Without Pain

"Aurora Winter gave one of the best presentations I have heard during my 16 years of teaching."

– **David K. Hensley**, Executive
Director, University of Iowa

"It's been just 7 weeks since my intensive mastermind with Aurora Winter where I made 4 videos, and my TV appearances have skyrocketed! I have been interviewed on 3 primary stations over 15 times in these 7 weeks, and they keep inviting me back. I encourage all of you to embrace Aurora's training. It works!"

– **Dr. Jennifer Herrera**, founder,
Tucson International Academies

ABOUT THE AUTHOR

AURORA WINTER, MBA, is the author of six books, including *Thought Leader Launch*. She has been featured by ABC-TV, CBS-TV, KTLA-TV, CBC-TV, Hallmark Channel, *Success* magazine, *Elle* magazine, *Maclean's* magazine, *The Huffington Post*, podcasts, and other media.

Aurora loves to be a catalyst for people to step into their greatness. She is the founder of Same Page, a publishing and training company that launches Thought Leaders.

The first step towards leadership is to release anything holding you back. Aurora and her team help emerging leaders transform setbacks into success.

The best way to build champions is to provide coaching and training. Using her expertise in business, neuroscience, and film, Aurora helps leaders discover, master, and monetize their message. As a result, her clients have raised millions, launched startups, delivered TEDx talks, written best-selling books, won awards, revitalized their lives, and appeared on TV, radio, and podcasts.

PLEASE POST A BOOK REVIEW

What was one thing you learned — or were reminded of—as a result of reading this book? What is one action you are now inspired to take? I would really appreciate it if you would let me know. Share a brief sentence as an online book review. This will help others discover this book, and it will make my day! Here is a link to make it quick and easy for you to find this book in Amazon or your preferred bookstore.

Please post a book review here:
https://books2read.com/launch.

Click on "Ratings" and then click on "Write a customer review." Reviews are important to a book's success. I look forward to reading your review and appreciate your time!

Let's connect readers!

Direct message me on www.LinkedIn.com/in/AuroraWinter or www.AuroraWinter.com.

FREE Thought Leader Launch starter library available for a limited time. Get it here today:

WWW.THOUGHTLEADERLAUNCH.COM

Made in the USA
Monee, IL
08 January 2021